COUNT CAVOUR.

A DISCOURSE

ON THE

LIFE, CHARACTER, AND POLICY

OF

COUNT CAVOUR,

DELIVERED IN THE HALL OF THE NEW YORK HISTORICAL SOCIETY,

February 20, 1862.

BY VINCENZO BOTTA, PH. D.,

PROFESSOR OF ITALIAN LITERATURE IN THE NEW YORK UNIVERSITY, LATE MEMBER OF THE PARLIAMENT, AND PROFESSOR OF PHILOSOPHY IN THE COLLEGES OF SARDINIA.

Vergine di servo encomio
E di codardo oltraggio,
Sorge or commosso al subito
Sparir di tanto raggio.
MANZONI.

NEW YORK:
G. P. PUTNAM, 532 BROADWAY,
1862.

C. A. ALVORD, PRINTFR.

DISCOURSE.

WHEN Pericles was called upon to deliver the funeral oration of those who had fallen in the first campaign of the Peloponnesian war, according to Thucydides, he began by extolling Athens, and having expatiated on her glories, her institutions, her laws, her sciences and arts, he concluded by exclaiming: "For such a republic, for such a country, the men whom we mourn fell and died." In meeting to do honor to the memory of Cavour, the most illustrious statesman of our time, if we were to follow the example of the Athenian orator, we could pay him no higher tribute than to dwell on the glories and calamities of the country which he was destined to restore to its nationality.

Enclosed by the great boundary of the Alps on one side, and encircled on the others by the sea, with an extensive coast indented with innumerable gulfs and bays, where the navies of the world might ride in safety, closely bordering on Africa, surrounded by a chain of islands, the natural highway and entrepot of commerce between Eastern and Western Europe, Italy seems to have been designated by the very hand of nature as the home of a great nation. Her people, the growth of ethnic varieties, long since, by the action of ages, moulded into one stock, speak substantially the same language, are nursed by the same literature, and bound together by the same civilization and historical associations. There is, perhaps, no country so strongly marked with the characteristics of a distinct individuality, and none whose individuality has been so long and so cruelly violated and crushed. First among the nations of Europe to emerge from the barbarism which succeeded the fall of the Roman empire, she shone forth through the darkness, a lonely star, in the splendor of her commerce, literature and arts, but she early became the victim of domestic feud and the coveted prey of foreign domination. While other countries, which centuries later had come forth from the mediæval chaos, were transforming themselves into national associations, their social elements clustering around their rising monarchies, Italy alone, although endowed with a more cohesive force, remained in a state of complete disorganization. The weakness of her feudal lords, the number of her municipalities, their jealousies, their wealth and vitality, and above all, the influence of the papacy and the empire, combined to resist the action of her affinities. For more than a thousand years, from the time when Charlemagne, in return for the imperial crown, granted to the Bishop of Rome immunity from his authority, Italy has been distracted by those two powers, whose long and bloody contests made her fertile plains one great battle-field, and her beautiful cities the scene of conspiracy, tumult and civil war, while their friendly alliances were no less hostile to her national existence.

As early as the 13th century, Dante called upon his countrymen to unite in the struggle for nationality. He seized the crude elements of the Italian language in the grasp of his mighty genius, and moulded it into a powerful engine of national thought. He embodied the history and the aspirations of Italy in the greatest monument of modern literature, made poetry the messenger of her sorrows and her hopes to coming generations, and the immortal voice which through the centuries called her forth to life. Following in his footsteps, Petrarch, whose fame, as a scholar, made him a power in the age in which he lived, addressed himself to popes, princes, and republics, entreated them to come to the rescue of the Italian people, and hailed the short-lived triumph of Rienzi, as the dawn of that day, when they were to be united under one government. Boccaccio, and the other tale writers of the 14th and 15th centuries, strove to undermine the papal authority, as one of the great impediments to national consolidation, and exposed to popular ridicule, under the garb of fiction, the vices against which Dante and Petrarch had before hurled their bitterest invectives. To this end of political unity Machiavelli particularly directed his labors as a writer and as a statesman, and more than once suffered imprisonment and torture. So with all the great representatives of Italian literature, from Dante to Alfieri, to Foscolo, Leopardi and Niccolini. The genius of Italy, taking its key-note from the bard of the Divine Comedy, has, through more than five hundred years, poured forth in lofty strains this perpetual aspiration of the Italians, echoing at the same time the mournful history of their divisions and bondage. But the voice of the muse had no spell to exorcise the evil spirits which presided over the destinies of the nation, and equally powerless were conspiracies, revolutions, and wars.

After the Congress of Vienna, with the restoration of the vassals of Austria on the thrones of the peninsula, the re-establishment of the Austrian predominance and the papal monarchy, for a short period overthrown by the first Napoleon, the chains of Italy seemed more firmly riveted than ever. But the master mind was soon to arise, which was to mould her scattered members into one whole, the great architect was soon to appear, who was to rear them into the sublime temple of national unity, founded on the corner-stone of constitutional liberty. It was reserved for Cavour to achieve, in a great measure, the work which the vain longings of an enslaved people and the heroic efforts of centuries had been unable to accomplish. It was reserved for him to inaugurate in Italy the policy of self-government, identical with that which has given rise to the great republic of these United States, to infuse new life into the country, which was the source of modern civilization, whose spirit flows through all modern society, as the blood of the mother flows through the veins of her offspring, and whose name sends a thrill of love and admiration through every heart which feels the power of what is beautiful and sublime. It is to the life of Cavour, as illustrated by his character and policy, that we now propose to direct our attention, a character and policy which, supported as he was by the enlightened patriotism and the heroic bravery of Victor Emmanuel, the generous friendship of Napoleon III., the almost fabulous achievements of Garibaldi, the moderation and energy of the Italian people, and the sympathy of civilized nations, led him to accomplish one of the greatest revolutions which history records.

Camillo Benso di Cavour was born in Turin, on the 10th of August, 1810, five years before the Congress of Vienna had concocted that conspiracy against the liberties of Italy, whose deadly effects, within less than half a century, he was destined to counteract by the boldness of his genius and the wisdom of his patriotism. He opened his eyes to the light, therefore, in the very capital of the kingdom of Sardinia, upon which the great mission of national regeneration was to devolve, and in the meridian of the power of the first Napoleon, in that memorable, although brief period of prosperity, which the country had attained under the influence of the French empire. He was descended from the noble family of the Bensi, whose origin dates back to the 12th century, and who having at a later period received the Marquisate of Cavour, were thenceforth designated by that name. His father, the Marquis Giuseppe Michele Benso di Cavour, was grand chamberlain of the Prince Borghese, governor of Piedmont, then under the sway of France, and his mother held the office of lady in waiting to the princess, the beautiful Pauline, sister of the first Napoleon. Camillo took his Christian name from the prince, who, with the princess, acted as sponsor in his baptism, and thus, ushered into the world under the auspices of the Bonapartes, we shall see him, in the course of a few years, welcome, as minister of Victor Emmanuel, the reappearance of that dynasty on the throne of France, and secure its alliance to the cause of Italian independence.

The early life of Cavour, like that of most men who leave their impression on the history of mankind, was a long and painful struggle, not from the absence of material prosperity, but from the antagonism in which he found himself with the prejudices of his time and the wretched condition of his country. It was in this crucible that his vigorous and inflexible nature was moulded, the breadth and the boldness of his character developed, and his individuality wrought out into its striking relief. His education began at that period when the restoration had brought back to Italy the old dynasties, with the petty and bigoted despotisms of the preceding age. Under the rule of the first Napoleon, important changes had been effected in Italy; feudal institutions had been swept away, civil and religious liberty introduced, and the latent power of the people roused to take part in the race of European progress. The former divisions of the territory, too, had almost entirely disappeared, or become merged into a sort of political individuality, based on the unity of legislation and administration, and on a thorough military organization. But now the country, again rent asunder and forced back under the double yoke of aristocratic and ecclesiastical authority, was again firmly chained to the thrones of Vienna and Rome.

No avenues to advancement but those of the army and the church being open, Camillo, like most of the young men of rank, was early sent to the Military Academy of Turin, for his education. He soon gave evidence of his precocious capacities, and when only ten years old was appointed a page to Charles Albert, then presumptive heir to the crown of Sardinia. This prince was at that time looked upon as the chief of the liberal party, and the appointment of the little Cavour was considered an act of opposition to the court, which regarded his family with marked coldness, on account of their former connection with the Bonapartes. The livery of the page, however, was ill suited to the instinctive independence which characterized him from his childhood, and he was soon discharged from his office, highly delighted "in having," as he expressed it, "thrown off his pack-saddle." He returned therefore to his studies at the Academy; but, owing to the prevailing methods of teaching, more calculated to disgust than to attract, he seems to have paid little attention to his lessons, and manifesting an equal distaste for boyish amusements, he spent his time in reading history and political treatises. But toward the close of the terms, he would put aside his favorite books, and in a few days prepare himself for the examinations, which he passed with such distinction, that at the age of sixteen he received his commission, and entered the army at eighteen, with the rank of lieutenant in the royal engineers. He was early employed in this capacity in important surveys and fortifications on the Apennines and the Alps, and in 1831 we find him engaged in similar works at Genoa. While in that city, having expressed himself with some freedom on political affairs, and his words being reported to the court, he was ordered for a year to the Fort of Bard, in the Valle di Aosta. On his release he resigned his commission. His character was no better fitted for the position of a military officer than for that of a page. The submission, silence and passive obedience required by military discipline, were not among his prominent qualities. Quick to discover the weakness and follies of those about him, unsparing in his trenchant wit and irony, proud and self-reliant, he was not born to obey, but to command.

Having thus freed himself from the trammels of his position, although with much opposition on the part of his father, Cavour now turned his whole attention to the political and social questions of the day, and began to prepare himself for that career of which, with the prescience of true genius, he had already some presentiment. In a letter written to a friend, who had condoled with him on his disgrace at the court, when only twenty-two years old, at the time when the prospects of Italy were little calculated to inspire hope, he expressed himself in the following remarkable words: "I thank you for the interest you take in my misfortune; but, believe me, I shall still accomplish my career in despite of it. I am a very, an enormously ambitious man, and when I am minister I shall justify my ambition; for I tell you, in my dreams I already see myself minister of the kingdom of Italy." In this intuitive belief that he was destined to play an important part in the future of his country, he now applied himself to the study of political science, and particularly of political economy, in which he took for his guide the writers of the great school founded by Adam Smith. He gathered from France and England books, reports, and other documents relating to finance, commerce and agriculture, and by untiring industry put scientific theories to the test of practical results.

Cavour watched with intense feeling the events of the French Revolution in 1830, the free trade and the reform agitation in England, in the hope that the progress which appeared to be in store for other nations, would be an omen of good for his countrymen. His letters of this time express his deep anxiety in behalf of Italy, and prove that his love for his country was of no late growth. "While all Europe," writes he, as early as December, 1829, to an English friend, "is walking with a firm step in the path of progress, unhappy Italy is always borne down under the same system of civil and religious tyranny. Pity those who, with souls made to develop the generous principles of civilization, are compelled to see their country brutalized by Austrian bayonets. Tell your countrymen, that we are not undeserving of liberty, that if we have rotten members, we have also men who are worthy to enjoy the blessings of light. Forgive me if I wander, but my soul is weighed down under the burden of indignation and of sorrow, and I feel a very sweet relief in thus opening myself to one who knows the causes of my grief, and surely sympathizes with them." And in another letter of July 1832, he continues to mourn the fate of his country as follows: "Pressed on one side by Austrian bayonets, on the other by the furious excommunications of the pope, our condition is truly deplorable. Every free exercise of thought, every generous sentiment is stifled, as if it were a sacrilege or a crime against the State. We cannot hope to obtain by ourselves any relief from such enormous misfortunes. The destiny of my countrymen, of the Romagna especially, is truly deplorable, and the steps which have been taken by the mediating powers, have only made it worse. The intervention of France is not even sufficient to exact the smallest reasonable concession from the pope. The voice of England alone, if raised in a firm and positive tone, can obtain for the people a supportable government, somewhat in harmony with the ideas and manners of our age."

On the accession of Charles Albert, the father of Cavour was appointed Vicario of Turin—a high office, which involved the charge of the police and the duty of watching the liberal party, and reporting its movements directly to the king. The marquis thus becoming the instrument of a petty and mistrustful government, although an amiable man in his private relations, brought upon himself a vast amount of popular odium, which extended to his family. Cavour himself was regarded with suspicion by the aristocratic class for his liberal views, and by the popular party for his aristocratic connections. Those only, whose lot it has been to drink silently drop by drop the bitter cup of moral constraint, whose hearts have been devoured by the slow fire of inward struggle, can measure the intensity of suffering to which his extremely sensitive nature must have been subjected by his early associations. Eager for distinction and power, yet obliged to endure the suspicions of all parties, attached by filial affection to him who was the principal instrument of the bigotry and the meanness of the government, he was forced to sacrifice on the altar of his penates the noblest aspirations of his youth. But let the old Vicario hunt down the friends of liberty, and slip his hordes to crush out every hope of freedom; under his own roof, born of his own flesh, a youth is fast approaching manhood, who shall soon scatter to the winds the engines of despotism, and, towering in moral stature far above all factions, open the pathway to the emancipation of his country. Millions, from Alps to Ætna, shall hail him as their leader, and follow him onward to the conquest of national liberty.

In 1833, Cavour travelled over various portions of the peninsula, and by actual observation made himself acquainted with its political and social condition. Even then it would seem that the Austrian authorities had a presentiment of the part which he was to play in the future of Italy, as an order was issued from the head-quarters of the police, to subject him to the most rigorous investigations on his entrance into Lombardy; "as there is reason," said the order, "to suspect that he may be the bearer of dangerous documents; for in spite of his youth he is already deeply corrupted in his political principles." In 1835, he visited Switzerland, the birthplace of his mother, and the residence of several of his relatives; and the intercourse which he ever after continued to hold with that republic, doubtless contributed to nurture his instinctive love of freedom. He left Geneva for Paris, from thence he passed over to England, a nation for which he expressed "that esteem and interest due to one of the greatest people that has done honor to the human race, a nation that has continually promoted the moral and material progress of the world, and whose civilizing mission is yet far from having reached its term."

Cavour regarded the English constitution with great admiration. He studied it thoroughly, and drew from it those broad principles of liberty, which characterize the Anglo-Saxon system of government, whether under the republican or monarchical form; principles which make the defence of individual rights the basis and the object of civil authority, and all interference of the State not demanded by the exigencies of social co-existence, an act of usurpation; which limit the action of the law to the security of the citizen, and lessening the power of the government enlarge the sphere of personal activity. He admired the robust individuality, the self-government, the personal independence and the self-reliance by which the Anglo-Saxon race is so distinguished, and that liberal spirit which has culminated in the electoral reform, the repeal of the corn-laws and the Catholic emancipation. That spirit which crossed the Atlantic in the Mayflower, expanded into higher perfection in these United States, and is at the present moment asserting itself more triumphantly than ever against the wanton attacks of its antagonist, which in the light of the 19th century, would perpetuate the reign of an oligarchy founded on human slavery.

But while the institutions of England and the United States are established on the principle of self-government, the nations of the European continent are organized on quite the opposite idea, the supremacy of the State over the citizen. There man is not free by nature, but receives his rights from law; there, whether in the monarchy of Louis XIV., in the schemes of Louis Blanc, or in those of Cabet, the State is the organizer of society, and the dispenser of liberty; there central authority assumes the responsibilities of the citizen, renders him, soul and body, dependent, absorbs municipal and provincial life, and becomes intolerant, monopolizing, and despotic. Crushed by the powerful machinery of the administration, the immortal sentiment of liberty must thus forever struggle, revolution must be a permanent condition, and the people continually vibrate between despotism and anarchy.

These two systems, in their nature and bearing, Cavour well understood, and his cordial devotion to the Anglo-Saxon idea of liberty inaugurated a new era in the policy of Europe. He was probably the first statesman of the continental nations who fully and practically appreciated the value of self-government; an appreciation which was the result of the comprehensiveness and independence of his mind, as well as of his extensive observation. During his residence in England, amidst the enjoyments of society, for which his connections, fortune and temperament afforded him every facility, he devoted himself to an earnest study of the working of the English constitution. He examined its effects on the social and commercial condition of the people, its influence on the production and distribution of wealth, commerce, private associations, mechanical inventions, improvements in manufactures and husbandry, charity schools and other benevolent institutions. At the same time he made himself master of the machinery of constitutional government, and acquainted with the rules of parliamentary proceedings. He was directed in this work of self-training by several prominent men of that country, and particularly by Mr. W. Brokerdon, with whom he had early contracted friendly relations, and whose varied talents as a mechanic, as a scholar and as an artist, peculiarly fitted him to guide the Italian student in his researches.

Cavour's admiration for England and her institutions, however, was by no means blind and undiscriminating; while he accepted in all its breadth the great prinçiple of constitutional liberty, and properly estimated the practical tendencies of the English people, he was unreserved in denouncing the English aristocracy for their neglect of the intellectual and moral requirements of the laboring classes, and he carefully excluded from the legislation of his country those features of the English law not strictly in accordance with the Italian character and the civilization of the present age.

In 1842, after an absence of several years, Cavour returned to Italy. He soon published various essays, both in Italian and French, remarkable for their comprehensive and liberal views. Among them that on "the State and Prospects of Ireland," received unqualified praise in England. He had visited that country, when the repeal agitation was at its height, and while he discouraged that movement, as utterly impracticable, he suggested many measures of redress for the grievances of the people, some of which have since been adopted. In that paper he bestows a well deserved eulogy on England, and in a masterly sketch of William Pitt, he shows a remarkable appreciation of the circumstances which led that statesman to pursue a line of policy which has been universally condemned. In his essay on "Communism" Cavour reduces its various questions to the problem: What is the rational principle to adopt in cases of conflict between the right of property, on which all social order depends, and the right of self-preservation and labor, which cannot be refused to any living man? Showing that these two rights have no absolute but only a relative worth, on one side he denounces communistic doctrines, as destructive of all individual liberty, as well as of all social organization, on the other he urges the wealthy classes to co-operate, by an enlightened benevolence, with the economists and philosophers, in lessening the evils arising from the unequal distribution of wealth. A high philosophical tone, a nice discrimination, logical deduction, and an earnest desire for the improvement of the people, are the principal characteristics of this treatise.

His essay on "Italian Railroads" is remarkable for its technical merits and the national point of view from which the subject is treated. Having indicated the most important lines for uniting the peninsula, as one condition of its independence, he concludes as follows: "Then railroads will stretch without interruption from the Alps to Sicily, and will cause all the obstacles and distances to disappear which separate the Italian people, and prevent them from forming a great and single nation." A few years later, when Italy entered upon the struggle for nationality, Cavour had the opportunity of carrying out his designs in this branch of the administration, and before his death the contracts were signed for the construction of numerous lines, which will soon embrace the whole country in their iron arms. In another essay on "the Influence of Commercial Reform in England on the Economical Condition of Italy," he shows the connection between political and economical advancement, urges the introduction of free institutions as a necessary condition for the commercial and industrial progress of the country, and expresses his unshaken faith in the talent, activity, and energy of the Italians, "which rendered their ancestors illustrious and powerful in the middle ages, when the Florentine and Lombard manufactures and the Genoese and Venetian fleets had no rivals in Europe," and which, if freed from the trammels of protectionism, would again raise Italy "to the first rank among the commercial nations of the world." He recommends, at the same time, the establishment of institutions of credit, scientific schools, and industrial associations, as the means of a rapid development for the various branches of industry, so wonderfully suited to the peculiarities of the soil, and insists on the duty of society to promote the material and moral welfare of the working classes, "who contribute most directly to the production of public wealth," which he declares, "ceases to be a real benefit to the country, unless the laborer derives an advantage from that increase." "Let us," he concludes, "develop those benevolent institutions, which are the honor of our past and present history, subjecting them to those scientific laws, the observance of which is essential in order to render institutions designed for the relief of human misery of real use and efficacy. Let us labor to enable our fellow-citizens, rich and poor, and the poor even more than the rich, to participate in the benefits of civil progress, and the increase of wealth. By so doing we shall solve peacefully, and like Christian men, the great social problem which others seek to solve by tremendous convulsions and awful disasters."

The years which intervened between his return home and the national revival of 1847, Cavour devoted to political researches, the improvement of his estates, and to all public and private enterprises calculated to promote the moral and material progress of the country. The establishment of infant asylums in Turin particularly engaged his attention, and he was early elected a member of the board of directors. But his interest in these institutions was regarded with so much jealousy by the court, that he was soon requested to resign his place, and to withdraw his name from the books of the association—a step which indicated at once his growing power and the weakness of the government. He was also one of the founders of the Agricultural Society of the State, through the papers of which he laid before his countrymen his enlarged and liberal views on trade and industry. The discussions on these topics led to others, involving still higher interests, and prepared the people for the political changes which were soon to follow.

We now reach the year 1847, when Italy seemed at last to awake to the consciousness of a new life. Although the national spirit since 1815 had been stifled, and almost extinguished, it had more than once burst forth in a fitful flame, too soon, however, to be again subdued and smothered. In 1831, a new apostle had appeared, who, burning with enthusiasm for liberty, had relighted the dying spark of nationality. Mazzini, from his exile, had continued for more than fifteen years to fan with unceasing activity the fire of patriotism in the hearts of his countrymen, to incite them to boldly throw off not only the yoke of foreign domination, but to cast aside every vestige of monarchical institutions, and to seek their national unity in one great republic. Fixed in this idea, he had subordinated the cause of independence to the introduction of republican government, as the only means adapted to sweep away the obstacles to the reconstruction of Italy, as a nation. The rulers of the country, wholly identified with the interests of the house of Hapsburg, had left to him no choice between national independence and their despotic sway, and from the beginning he had frowned on all compromises with the thrones of the peninsula, and directed his efforts to their overthrow. Proceeding, however, upon an imaginary estimate of the strength of the country, ignoring the actual condition of human nature, and the exigencies of European policy, commanding but limited means, entirely disproportioned to his object, and led on by his instinct, the bold conspirator was destined to exhaust his party in a series of attempts, which, though protests against despotism, were little calculated to produce those national results to which his life was devoted.

Cavour regarded the projects of Mazzini as utterly powerless to lighten the burden of domestic rule and to emancipate the country from foreign domination. A practical man by nature, and a statesman of the school which acknowledges Machiavelli as its founder, and Richelieu and Burke as its great representatives, his policy was not engendered in the secret chambers of conspiracy, but was moulded on a comprehensive knowledge of the forces which patriotism could command, and on the just appreciation of the necessity of the time. Accordingly he believed that the conquest of nationality could only be effected through the harmonizing of many antagonistic interests, and the combination of many clashing tendencies, the control of which depended entirely on slow, patient, and steady action. From the first appearance of Mazzini, he had not only refused to take any part in his futile and spasmodic efforts, but he had unreservedly discouraged and condemned his policy, as antinational, and big with calamities. Regarding the growth of public sentiment as the true regenerative force, he now hailed with delight the favor with which the more conservative views of Cesare Balbo, Massimo d'Azeglio, and Vincenzo Gioberti were received.

These writers, however discordant in minor points, all agreed in urging upon their countrymen the necessity of radically changing the method of revolutionary action, of doing away with all secret conspiracies, and of openly laboring for the attainment of national independence. They strove to enlist in the cause the interest and ambition of the Italian princes, and insisted on the possibility of a compact between them and the States, by which the rulers were to grant concessions calculated to infuse new life into the country, and the people to extend to them the tenure of their power. Had the princes followed that course, they would have been thrown into the onward current, and, soon separated from Austria, they would have been forced into a confederation in order to protect themselves from the common enemy, who, sooner or later, would have been expelled from the peninsula. So while Mazzini struggled for nationality, by attempting to establish a republic—an enterprise rendered impossible by the condition of Europe and Italy herself—the chiefs of the new party proposed to accomplish the same object through the existing monarchy, renovated, however, by constitutional liberty.

Prominent among those leaders was Gioberti. A man of lofty patriotism and saintly character, a philosophical writer of great renown, distinguished by depth, breadth, and novelty of thought, as well as by brilliancy of style, his influence was powerful and salutary. Considering the papal and the Austrian governments as the two main stumbling-blocks to Italian independence, in his works he aimed at the overthrow of both. The papacy he did not directly attack, as his predecessors in philosophy had done, but he attempted to flank and turn it into the service of the nation. He sketched an Ideal, youthful and vigorous, which he endeavored to assimilate to the old and worn-out institution of the Vatican, and to place at the head of the Italian movement. The appearance of Pius IX. in the garb of a reformer, seemed for a moment to reduce his theory to fact, though in reality it rendered the discrepancies and incongruities between the ideal and the real papacy more conspicuous and irreconcilable. Could we lose sight of the earnestness and sincerity of Gioberti's character, it would appear that in describing the papal power as the great regenerating agency of our age, he intended rather to satirize than to defend its pretensions, and that he aimed to effect by praise what its professed opponents strove to accomplish by open attack. Thus only could we explain the contradictions exhibited in his life and works, and understand how, an ardent professor of the papal faith, he could undermine its foundation bys ubstituting private judgment for submissive belief; how, an extravagant eulogist of the church, he could be an unrelenting censor of its institutions and laws, and particularly a stern denouncer of the Jesuits, the acknowledged exponents of its doctrine; how, finally, an enthusiastic admirer of the papal hierarchy, he could abandon the papal priesthood as a calling inconsistent with his independence as a philosopher, as well as with his duties as a citizen. It is only by regarding his philosophy in reference to his political objects, that we are able to do it full justice; for when Pius IX. abandoned the Italian cause, which as pope he could not consistently support, Gioberti, leaving at once the papacy to its own destiny, sought other more substantial bases for national existence, and pointed out the house of Savoy as the only hope of Italy. He accordingly, as early as 1851, in his last and best work: "Il Rinnovamento civile d'Italia," established on scientific grounds the national hegemony of Sardinia, and showed the necessity of the French alliance, and the consolidation of the whole nation under the sceptre of Victor Emmanuel, foreshadowing the glorious events, whose consummation, alas! he was not destined to behold. Whatever, therefore, may be the philosophical value of Gioberti's opinions, his political services undoubtedly paved the way to the bold and brilliant career of Cavour.

The project of an Italian confederacy, under the nominal presidency of the pope, and the actual leadership of Sardinia being the only form of national existence which at that time appeared practicable, was accepted by Cavour, and he shaped his policy accordingly, giving, however, but little importance to the papal element. When the censorship of the press was somewhat relaxed, he established in Turin, in connection with Cesare Balbo and others, the "Risorgimento," a daily paper of which he became the chief editor, and which, owing to his skilful management, exerted a great influence on the course of events. In this paper he advocated the independence of Italy, union between the princes and people, progressive reform, and a confederation of the Italian States; he developed, also, those more general principles of free government which he afterward carried out in his administration. In accordance with the same principles, he also signed about this time a petition to Ferdinand of Naples, imploring him to second the progressive movement, little thinking that the events of the next few years would place at his disposal the crown of the descendant of that miscreant king.

In the beginning of 1848 Cavour took the still more important step of demanding from Charles Albert a constitution for his native State, till then under absolute sway. A deputation from Genoa had come to Turin to urge upon the king the expulsion of the Jesuits, and the organization of the national militia; and the chief editors, aware of the dangers with which that agitation was fraught, met together for the purpose of combining their action in support of that demand. Cavour took no part in the proceedings until the assembly was called to decide upon the course of their future action; when, coming boldly to the point, he said: "Why should we ask in this roundabout way for paltry reforms which will end in little or no good? Let us at once petition the king to grant us the benefit of free discussion, in which the opinions, the interests, and the wants of the people may be represented. Let us demand a constitutional charter." The boldness of this motion was the more striking, since, owing to the unpopularity from which he had not even yet emerged, he could rely very little on the support of his colleagues, and still less on the favor of the king. Whether Charles Albert was a despot by nature, or whether he assumed only the garb of despotism to make himself acceptable to Austria, and thus blind her to his future designs, he was extremely jealous of his own power, and very far from admitting the right of the people to share with him the management of their own affairs. He had, indeed, under the pressure of the times, reluctantly granted a few administrative reforms; and now that a private citizen, the target of both the reactionary and progressive parties, should dare loudly to demand a representative government, and thus divide his sovereignty, was such a monstrous assumption, that but for the agitations of the times, Cavour would have been at once disgraced. The majority of his colleagues having declined to support his motion, and the censors of the press not having allowed the publication of the proceedings of the meeting, he took upon himself to write directly to the king, informing him of what had passed, explaining his motives, and pointing out the dangers involved in a further delay to comply with the exigencies of the age.

Whatever may have been the effect of this communication, it is certain that the constitution was soon after granted, and he who was first to demand it was, within a few years, called to mould it into the corner-stone of the liberties of the whole Italian people. Had Charles Albert longer resisted the advancing tide of public opinion, his dynasty would, in all probability, have been swept away with those of the other rulers; as it was, the charter thus timely granted proved to be the fortunate bark destined to bear his successor triumphantly amidst contending storms to the throne of Italy.

Cavour was now appointed member of a committee charged with the drawing up of the electoral bill, a labor which devolved chiefly upon him. This bill was so broad and liberal in its principles, that it proved not only adapted to the wants of Sardinia, but it has since been extended to the whole united kingdom.

The dawn of Italian independence now approaches. Milan has risen in arms, and driven the Austrian troops beyond her gates. The expectant nation waits only for a chieftain to rout the enemy from his strongholds, and pursue him beyond the Alps. To Charles Albert all eyes are turned, all arms are extended. But he hesitates, and fears to risk the crown he wears for the more brilliant one which he would grasp. While his chivalrous character, his ambition, the traditions of the house of Savoy, urge him onward, his family connections, his conservative tendencies, his dread of revolution, hold him back. His advisers recoil from the responsibility of plunging the little State of Sardinia into a war with a powerful empire, and the destiny of the nation seems equally imperilled by action and delay. But with Cavour in this crisis there was no doubt, no hesitation; and while the king, surrounded by his counsellors, was debating instead of marching at the head of his army, he published the following appeal to arms: "The supreme hour for the monarchy of Savoy has struck; the hour for intrepid action; the hour on which depends the fate of empires and the destiny of nations. In view of the late events, there is no time for doubt or delay; of all policies such would be the most fatal. Cool in judgment, and accustomed to listen rather to the suggestions of reason than to the promptings of the heart, well weighing every word which we utter, we solemnly and conscientiously declare, that there is only one course to be pursued for the king, the government, and the nation. War! war at once and without delay. It is impossible to retreat. The nation is already at war with Austria. It is rising now to the aid of the Lombards. Our volunteers have already crossed the frontier; our citizens are furnishing ammunition to the Milanese. The peace with Austria is broken, and the old treaties on either side are torn and trampled underfoot. We have not to decide whether we shall commence war or not; our sole option is, whether we shall declare ourselves loyally and boldly for the cause of humanity and Italy, or whether we shall follow for a period the tortuous path of a doubtful and insincere policy. We are in a position in which courage is the true prudence, and temerity wiser than caution. Lombardy is in flames; Milan is besieged; there is nothing left for us but to fly to the aid of our brothers. Had we but five thousand men on the frontier, we should march them at once to Milan. They might be defeated; but the moral effect of such an expedition would aid the Italian cause far more than a defeat could do it injury. Woe to us if, for the sake of increasing our preparations, we should come too late; if, when we are ready to cross the Ticino, we should hear that the queen of Lombardy has fallen! In our position there is but one policy, we repeat; not that of a Louis Philippe and Guizot, but that of a Frederick the Great, a Napoleon, and a Charles Emmanuel; the great policy of bold counsels."

The same day on which Cavour expressed such a decided opinion on the great question of the intervention in Lombardy, Charles Albert issued the famous proclamation by which he placed himself at the head of the revolution, and secured for the State the leadership of the nation. Occupying a commanding position between the Alps and the Mediterranean, inhabited by a people distinguished by their practical sense, vigor of character, and warlike spirit, and ruled by a dynasty whose power in Italy had been gradually augmented during eight centuries, Sardinia seemed peculiarly fitted for the destiny assigned her. From this time she made common cause with the whole nation; and bravely entering into the arena, staked her own existence on the issue. Twice prostrated, she twice arose from the conflict; and at last, under the guidance of Cavour, we shall behold her uniting the long divided provinces into one whole, as a nebulous spot scarcely visible far in the space above, attracting around its nucleus masses of cosmical vapor, at length becomes a luminous star.

During the war of 1848, Turin witnessed the opening of the first parliament. In that session Cavour sat as the deputy of the first district of his native city; a constituency which, with the exception of one short session, he continued to represent to the last. United to the aristocracy by birth and by early associations, yet separated from that class by his liberal views; tending toward the democratic party in his progressive ideas, yet opposing all radical and visionary schemes, he at first stood almost alone in the chamber, an isolated, yet remarkable figure. Although he gave his cordial support to the administration, headed by his friend Cesare Balbo, he did not shrink, even in his maiden speech, from rebuking the ministry for their weakness and indecision in conducting the war, at a time when the only hope for its success was in bold and vigorous measures. He urged the immediate and unconditional annexation of Lombardy and Venetia to Sardinia, as a necessary step to strengthen the national forces; and, devoted to constitutional freedom, he opposed all efforts to curtail it, even such as the exigency of the time might seem to justify. He now began to give evidence of his financial abilities, and otherwise showed himself to be eminently endowed with those qualities which belong to the genuine statesman and the leader in parliamentary debate.

When the news reached Turin of the defeat of the Sardinian army on the plains of Custoza, Cavour at once enlisted as a private volunteer, and was only restrained from taking the field by the armistice of Salasco, which for the time put an end to the war. He continued therefore to sit in parliament, using now all his influence to secure, through the mediation of England and France, an honorable peace with Austria, since he considered it impossible at that time to carry on the contest.

Whatever opinion may then have been entertained of Cavour's policy, it cannot be denied that it was eminently practical, and dictated by that enlightened statesmanship which, in the pursuit of an object, knows how to delay movements or change positions in order to secure its future attainment. Thus he opposed in 1849 the bolder views of Gioberti, which he regarded as endangering the national cause at home and abroad; but when Gioberti, alarmed at the excesses of the liberal party in central Italy, proposed the armed intervention of Sardinia to restore the exiled princes under the guaranty of constitutional liberty, he found a staunch supporter in Cavour. Again, when the defeat of that measure led the prime minister to withdraw from the cabinet, and war was once more declared by the succeeding administration, he did not hesitate to bring all his influence to the support of the government, although to the last he had discouraged the renewal of hostilities. So the true statesman rises superior to party, and readily sacrifices personal opinions and feelings on the altar of patriotism.

The course pursued by Cavour during those stormy years exhibits in strong relief that moral courage with which he was peculiarly endowed. Believing the democratic tendencies of the time utterly ruinous to the national cause, he fearlessly threw himself against the prevailing current of opinion, and thus greatly increased his unpopularity. But this could not deter him from performing what he considered his duty; for he did not belong to that class of politicians to be found everywhere, whose love of country is subservient to self-interest, and whose object is confined to flattering popular passions and prejudices. It was a striking spectacle to see him at that time from his seat in the chamber defying the storm of hisses and yells with which he was frequently assailed from the galleries. Often he called them to order, or moved that they should be cleared according to the rules. "I am not to be prevented from speaking," said he on one occasion, "by shouts and hisses. What I believe to be true, that will I speak out. If you compel me to silence, you insult not me alone, but the chamber. And now I shall proceed." And with his usual self-possession he resumed his discourse.

The disasters of 1848 and '49 were mainly owing to the want of unity in the pursuit of national independence. As the first campaign had failed through the defection of Pius IX. and other princes, the misfortunes of the second were chiefly due to the attempts of the minority to introduce republican governments into some of the States. Whatever may be thought of the relative value of republican or monarchical institutions abstractly considered, it can hardly be questioned that such an experiment was at that time highly impolitic. With Charles Albert supported by the sole army in the peninsula; with the constitutional party predominant in number as well as in intelligence and social position; with the nation surrounded by jealous and powerful monarchies, and France fast drifting toward the empire, to venture on such a course was to divide the people into distracting factions, and to draw upon the country the armies of Europe. So Italy fell; on the plains of Novara, on the lagoons of Venice, within the walls of her ancient capital, she was defeated because she was not united; because, while Turin was fighting for the common cause, Naples and Palermo bowed under the iron yoke of the Bourbon, and Rome and Florence allowed themselves to be led astray by the mad hallucinations of Mazzini. With Italy, Sardinia was crushed; she saw her king, in disguise, pass through the camp of the enemy on his way to exile; her standards trailed in the dust, the stronghold of Alessandria garrisoned by the Austrians, her army almost destroyed, her finances ruined, her commerce obstructed, her people distracted, her very existence imperilled.

Such was the condition of Sardinia when Victor Emmanuel ascended the throne. Although known as an intrepid soldier, he was by no means a favorite with the people, educated as he had been in an atmosphere of narrow, despotic, and bigoted influences; and the disaster of Novara had not lessened the unfavorable impression under which he came into power. Mistrusted by the country, the State disorganized, a large section of the liberal party in tumult, the army discontented, and Austrian power in the ascendant, there was reason to fear that the inexperienced king would furl the national flag, abolish constitutional liberty, and shape his course in accordance with that of the other sovereigns. But Victor Emmanuel was not the man to sacrifice the great interests at stake. On the fatal night of Novara, when Charles Albert, having in vain sought an honorable death at the hand of the enemy, surrounded by his generals, resigned his crown, the young king had unsheathed his sword, and, brandishing it toward the Austrian camp, had sworn to avenge the wrongs of Italy. Generous and fearless, Victor Emmanuel did not shrink from the dangers by which he was encompassed, and from his accession he resolved to walk in the footsteps of his father, to uphold the free institutions of the state, and retain the leadership of the nation.

To this end he not only pledged his word before the parliament, but he intrusted himself and the administration of the country to Massimo d'Azeglio, whose name alone was a symbol of nationality. No man represented the cause more entirely, and none was more fitted to guide the State through that dangerous period. Though born in Turin, he had passed his life chiefly in Rome and Florence, and from the study of Italian history, literature and art, he had derived that national character by which his career has been so singularly marked. In all the manifestations of his wonderfully versatile genius, as a painter of European renown, as a novelist scarcely inferior to Manzoni and Grossi, as an able political writer and a gallant soldier, Italy had been to him what Beatrice was to Dante and Laura to Petrarch. She was his muse when, uniting history and poetry to art, with master hand which recalls the genius of Salvator Rosa, he depicted on canvas the challenge of Barletta, the toast of Ferruccio, the battles of Legnano, of Turin, and the Assietta; and when, with surpassing wealth of imagination, he illustrated the marvellous fancies of Ariosto, as Michael Angelo had before delineated those of Dante. Italy still inspired him when, elevating romantic fiction to its highest expression, he evoked from the past the heroes of history, and with glowing ardor in his Ettore Fieramosca and Nicolò de Lapi, he portrayed the varying features of patriotism in the strife of the battle-field or in the contending emotions of love. And so, too, when, in the "Casi di Romagna" and the "Lutti di Lombardia," he exposed the iniquities of the courts of Rome and Vienna, which had lighted insurrections in those provinces only to extinguish them in blood, and warned his countrymen against the reckless agitators who were their dupes and tools. In 1848 Azeglio had laid aside the pencil and the pen for the sword; he had fought gallantly and had been wounded on the field; and thus prepared both by thought and action, on the accession of Victor Emmanuel he was called to the premiership of the cabinet. His high moral nature, his earnestness, his accomplishments, the simplicity and the refinement of his manners, softened by the influence of literature and the arts, his eloquence, and his devotion to the country, endeared him to the people; while his aristocratic connections, his well-known moderation and prudence, and his open opposition to the Mazzini party, rendered him acceptable to the courts of Europe.

At that time European nations were fast tending toward military despotism, and the conquests of the preceding year were passing from the grasp of the people. The bastard republic of France had not only refused aid to the war of Italian independence, but she had armed her troops against the sister republic of Rome; the lion of St. Mark, after a heroic resistance, had fallen again beneath the blood-stained talons of the double-headed eagle; Messina and Palermo had been bombarded; Naples, misled by the treacherous designs of her tyrant, had seen her streets flow with the blood of her citizens; and Florence, even the beautiful Florence, birthplace and shrine of Italian genius, had been polluted by the hated presence of the Austrian troops. While despotism in Italy again held its carnival, the sun of liberty, which had shone with fitful gleams in Hungary, now again set in darkness; Germany sank once more to her former dreams and abstractions; and France, startled at her own advance, was fast falling beneath a military dictatorship. In the midst of these opposing forces, Sardinia, in which were centred the hopes of all Italy, was forced to take her course, a frail bark on a stormy sea, struck on all sides by the wings of the tempest, and trembling on the breakers which threatened to engulf her. But Azeglio is at the helm, and under his guidance the bark shall safely outride the storm. When reaction menaced the only free State of the peninsula, and the republicans, by their futile attempts at revolution, seemed bent on precipitating a crisis that would involve the armed intervention of Europe, the constitutional party stood by Azeglio, and opposed the enemies of the constitution both at home and abroad. Thus Sardinia was saved from the dire calamities prepared for her by the conspiracies concocted at the same time and for the same purpose in the cabinets of diplomacy and in the secret councils of agitators.

The constitutional party found in Cavour its most powerful and devoted supporter. But while he coincided with Azeglio in his efforts to preserve free institutions, differences of opinion soon arose between those two statesmen as to the policy to be pursued. The administration, in view of the dangers from abroad, regarded a strict conservatism as best calculated to avert them; Cavour, on the contrary, while he dreaded reaction equally with his friend, dreaded still more the lethargy which this policy would necessarily induce, and believed that a more liberal course, without endangering relations with foreign governments, would endear Sardinia to the progressive party abroad, satisfy the demands of public opinion, and more firmly attach the Italian people to the house of Savoy. Hence, when the storm had somewhat subsided, he at once urged upon the government more progressive measures.

The war of independence immediately following the promulgation of the constitution, had thus far prevented the parliament from introducing into legislation those reforms which lay potentially within its provisions. So that, although endowed with this charter of rights, the people continued to be ruled in many respects by the laws of the former regime. Sardinia had sealed, with the blood of her sons, her claim to the leadership of the national cause, but the merit of that claim was yet to be proved by the wisdom of her codes; the flag of Italian liberty proudly waved on the Carignano palace, but it waved as yet over a people who still dragged the chains of their former thraldom. To throw off these chains, to bring the legislation in accordance with the constitution, to disengage the State from the clutches of the church, to give full expansion to the principles of liberty, was, according to Cavour, the only course for Sardinia to pursue, if she desired to be worthy of the championship of Italy.

This task, beset with extraordinary difficulties, required energy and boldness, as well as extensive knowledge of economic and political science; and while Azeglio was more able to guide the State safely through the dangers from abroad, Cavour was better fitted for the work of internal reform. The patriotism of the former was more spontaneous and instinctive; that of the latter the result of reflection and study; and in this regard Azeglio more resembled Mazzini than Cavour. But while Mazzini, without calculation or discrimination, recklessly abandoned himself to his instincts, and wasted his energies in spasmodic efforts, the fine judgment and the tact of Azeglio, mingled with excessive caution, impelled him in an opposite direction. A true artist as a painter and as a writer, he was also an artist as a statesman. The idea of liberty produced in his mind the effect of the beautiful; feeling it keenly rather than understanding it comprehensively, he fell in love with it, he strove to actualize it, but finding himself powerless to give it complete expression, he abandoned himself to its contemplation. Cavour, on the contrary, had no taste for the arts, and, a thoroughly business man, dealt with political questions as with practical concerns. Without wasting himself in looking at the ideal side of political issues, he strove to attain practical results. The mind of Azeglio was more of an oriental cast; the characteristics of Cavour were those of the genuine Yankee. Had they lived in the age of chivalry, the one would have been a knight of the crusades, the other the builder of the river-dykes of Lombardy; or had they made a pilgrimage to the East, while the one would have returned laden with relics, the other would have brought back a cargo of merchandise. These differences manifested themselves even in their early life; the young Azeglio leaves a luxurious home, and with scanty means proceeds to Rome to study the arts; Cavour, on the contrary, delays his travels abroad to look after his estates, and by his wonderful business talent largely increases his ample fortune. Vastly surpassed by Azeglio in æsthetic attainments, Cavour towered over him in extent of knowledge, comprehensiveness of intellect, quickness of perception, force of character, and energy of action; and while the one in great crises advanced timidly and slowly, feeling his way, the other, with his object clearly in view, and the full consciousness of his power, overleaped all impediments. These peculiarities in the character of the two statesmen nature had impressed even on their external appearance. The slender form, the delicate features, and the poetical expression of Azeglio marked him as a man of refined sensibility and romantic sentiment, as the keen eye, the broad brow, and the sturdy figure of Cavour, indicated at once the iron will and the power to enforce it.

The first step toward reform was, to emancipate the State from the church, to disengage it from the ecclesiastical power, which for so many ages had penetrated and incrusted every department, and clogged and prevented all progress. Azeglio would gladly have put an end to the usurpations, immunities, and privileges of the clergy; yet his lack of knowledge in ecclesiastical matters, his caution, and his taste, made him shrink from entering into a contest so bitter and uncongenial; and, pressed by public opinion, he strove to obtain by negotiation that which he lacked the vigor to take by force. He had again and again appealed to the holy see, had sent envoy after envoy, written long diplomatic dispatches interlarded with quotations from the Scriptures, the fathers, and the councils, humbly imploring the pope to allow himself to be shorn of his power, and striving to show to the infallible head of the church what a monstrous blunder he was committing in refusing the request. Unsuccessful in this, he had placed on the head of the young king, accustomed only to the helmet of the warrior, the cap of the theologian, and drew the sovereign into a personal controversy with the pope, who, in all questions relating to his own authority, has ever regarded discussion as impertinence. The statesman who held the reins of the government had yet to learn that the Gordian knot must be cut by a bold stroke. Had England in the 16th century waited for the pleasure of the court of Rome to break loose from its yoke, she would yet find herself at the very threshold of civilization. Had Louis IX., Charles VII., and Louis XIV., demanded the previous consent of the pope, the pragmatic sanctions which almost entirely freed France from the authority of Rome would never have been promulgated. Had the first Napoleon failed to impose his own conditions, his concordat would never have been signed. It is useless for Spartacus to kneel before his master, to discuss or to compromise; for his liberty he must boldly strike.

Cavour urged upon Azeglio the necessity of more vigorous measures. He pointed out the impossibility of reconciling the exigencies of the present civilization with an institution of the past, and the fallacy of contending that the pope had no right to interfere in the legislation of the State, while that right was admitted by imploring him to relinquish it. Owing to his influence Count Sicardi was called to the cabinet, which was thus strengthened by the upright and fearless character of that statesman, by his profound knowledge of jurisprudence, and the fame which he enjoyed as the advocate of the views of Paolo Sarpi, the able and bold defender of the independence of

Venice against papal encroachments in the 17th century. The first measure of this minister was the introduction of a bill by which ecclesiastical courts and immunities were at once abolished, the clergy were subjected to the common law, religious corporations were prohibited from accepting donations or bequests, and other provisions calculated to check the ecclesiastical predominance were proposed. Although this bill embraced only a few of the needed reforms, it involved the great principle of the independence of the State from the church, and as such it obtained on one side the unqualified approval of the liberal party, on the other it was met by the church faction with an animosity which could not have been more bitter had it at one stroke put an end to all papal usurpations.

Cavour supported the bill of Sicardi in a speech remarkable for its comprehensive grasp of thought, and the power with which his views were enforced. Advocating a progressive policy, he thus addressed the administration on that occasion: "Go on boldly, then, in the path of reform. Do not hesitate because you are told that the time is inexpedient; do not fear lest you should weaken the constitutional monarchy intrusted to your charge. Instead of weakening it, you will cause it to take such firm root in the country, that even if the storm of revolution should arise around us, the monarchy will not only not succumb to the onslaught, but, collecting around it all the vital forces of Italy, will lead our nation to the lofty destiny prepared for her." His speech, which greatly contributed to the passage of the bill, met with passionate opposition from many of his political associates, who from this time regarded him with bitter aversion. But, heeding neither remonstrance nor accusation, he pursued his onward course, though friends and party remained behind. In a subsequent speech he developed a complete system of reform in all the different branches of government, with such extraordinary power as to attract universal attention, and to establish his position as the first statesman in the country.

In the autumn of 1850, on the death of Count Santa Rosa,

Cavour was named his successor as minister of agricultural and commercial affairs; he was soon after charged with the department of the navy, and later with the still more important one of finance. It is said that when his appointment was suggested by Azeglio to the king, he remarked with striking foresight: "It is very well, but this man will soon supplant you all;" and indeed Cavour was not long in the cabinet, before he became its ruling spirit. He was scarcely seated in his ministerial chair before he made overtures to all the principal governments of Europe, which soon resulted in commercial treaties with England, France, Belgium, Sweden, Denmark, the Zollverein, Switzerland, Holland, and even with Austria; he strove to open new avenues to commerce, planted a consulate wherever he could send a ship, and urged the establishment of a line of steamers between the Mediterranean and the two Americas; a favorite project with him, for which as early as 1853 he secured from the parliament liberal pecuniary aid. Although this scheme failed through unforeseen obstacles, it is to be hoped that at a no distant period it will be successfully carried out, particularly in view of the new conditions of the peninsula. The country which gave birth to Columbus demands a closer connection with the New World.

Convinced that the nation most generous in commercial treaties is in the end the gainer, a passionate admirer of Adam Smith, Ricardo, and Robert Peel, and from the first an advocate of the principles of free trade, Cavour at once set to work to introduce them into practice, and lowered or abolished the tariff on importations in favor of those countries which would reciprocate with Sardinia. In this manner he intended to increase indirectly the revenue of the State, to promote individual wealth, and by forcing his countrymen into competition with nations more advanced, to rouse them from that lethargy which was equally fatal to their material interests and to their political and moral character. Indeed, free trade became in the hands of Cavour a political engine as well as an economical principle; and by making Sardinia a free market, and connecting her with the commerce of other nations, he rendered her expansion and prosperity an object of interest to them all. In carrying out this policy he was bitterly opposed, not only by the reactionary party, but by many friends of progress, who, unable to rise to his high stand-point, demanded protection for agricultural productions, and denounced commercial liberty as ruinous alike to the independence and the prosperity of the country. The opposition was carried so far as finally to end in a challenge from one of his most violent adversaries. On this occasion he exhibited his usual courage and calmness. Immediately before the meeting took place, he delivered in the chamber a long speech on the subject under discussion, and then, with the same composure which attended his ordinary movements, repaired to the appointed place. The combatants fired at twenty-five paces, but both were unhurt, and the affair terminated.

But no provocation, no denunciation, no danger, could divert Cavour from his course, while he beheld in the distance the magnificent results of his policy. By sacrificing high duties, he encouraged importation, and gave a new impulse to industry and to revenue. The importations of 1858, as compared with those of 1855, augmented more than fifty per cent.; the exportations in still greater proportion. The growth and manufacture of silk increased three-fold, the cotton manufacture five-fold, and so, more or less, with wool, flax, machinery, and the like. The principle of free trade has probably nowhere been so successfully tested as in Sardinia, although it had its first trial at a time when the resources of the country were crippled by two disastrous wars, by mysterious diseases which long affected the two great staples, silkworms and vines, and by various commercial crises in Europe and America.

To Cavour Sardinia is also chiefly indebted for the network of railroads which furrows her territory. When he entered the cabinet there were scarcely one hundred miles in the country, and at the time of his death all the principal lines in that part of the kingdom were in full operation. To expedite the public works, he early called to the cabinet the eminent engineer

Paleocapa, through whose industry he soon completed the road between Turin and Genoa, which from its mountainous character presented obstacles almost insurmountable. To this great trunk branches were added, connecting those two cities with the other main points of the State, with the valley of the Danube and eastern Europe, with Switzerland and Germany by proposed tunnels through the northern Alps, and with France and England by that colossal work now in progress, that is to pierce Mount Cenis, to open within the next five years the gloomy corridors of the Alps to the locomotive, and afford to western Europe through Italy the most direct passage to the east. With equally enlightened views he established telegraphic communication in all directions; and having united Turin to the other cities of the State and to the capitals of Europe by the magic wire, he extended it through the sea, and from Piazza Castello sent his orders to Cagliari and Sassari, and his greetings to Malta and Africa.

The transfer of the naval arsenal to the Gulf of Spezia was also a favorite plan with him, which, when accomplished, will afford the navy one of the most splendid harbors in the world, and facilitate those improvements in the port of Genoa calculated to render it a fit emporium for cosmopolitan commerce.

When to this we add the increase of the army and navy, the construction of fortifications and men-of-war, the transformation of sailing vessels into steam frigates, the extraordinary development of the mercantile marine, the establishment of institutions of public credit, the expansion of the national bank, the abolition of the legal rate of interest, the reduction of postage, the extension of popular and technical education, and many other reforms, which he carried out either directly through his personal exertions or indirectly through his influence and supervision, we may form an idea of the colossal work which he accomplished in the period which intervened between 1851 and 1859.

Of course, in the execution of his vast designs Cavour was forced to increase taxation; and that he failed to reform this important department has been a general charge against his administration. But, considering the extraordinary and perplexing circumstances in which he found himself, the wants of the country and the means at hand, we hold it as not the least evidence of his practical wisdom that he, although urged on by popular demand, knew how to abstain from innovations which even in ordinary times are fraught with danger. To augment existing taxes and to introduce new ones is, after all, the system which is followed in the great crises of all countries, and a better method is yet to be devised for supplying the ways and means of governments. So it is with public debt. Taxation and debt are but relative terms corresponding to public wealth; and to estimate the burden of a nation, its resources must be taken into account. If Cavour has enormously increased the liabilities of his country, he has in a greater proportion augmented its assets. England in the 16th century had no public debt, and her taxation was but one-fortieth of what it is now; the United States at the epoch of the declaration of independence had no debt, and but little taxation; yet it will hardly be said that the economical condition of those countries in the past was better than at the present time. Moreover, and this point should never be overlooked, it was necessary that Sardinia should advance the means requisite for the deliverance of Italy, and no pecuniary consideration could restrain that State from the fulfilment of its duty. It was owing to the financial reputation of Cavour that its public credit was sustained amidst the most trying circumstances, and that the country was thus enabled to support the burden of the national struggle. While Russia, Austria, and other great powers found insurmountable difficulties in raising money, Sardinia, although suffering from the cholera and deficient harvests, never failed to negotiate her loans in London and Paris at the market price, and her bonds, issued under the authority of her great statesman, have at all times been as marketable in the exchanges of those capitals as the United States coupons are in Wall street.

It was only one year from the time when Cavour entered the

cabinet, and so vigorously commenced the work of retrieving the country from its prostrate condition, when the night of the 2d of December, 1851, closed upon the grave of the French republic. Three years before the coup d'état took place, pointing out the dangers by which France was menaced, Cavour had predicted in so many words that the socialistic tendencies which then prevailed would bring the nephew of the great emperor to the imperial throne. At the time when Louis Napoleon seized with a strong hand the reins of power, France was suffering from the effects of the excessive impulse given by the government of Louis Philippe to the interests of the wealthy at the expense of the laboring classes. Capital had absorbed all the advantages of labor, and held over it despotic sway. A universal uneasiness arose, mingled with a deep hatred toward those whom the people regarded as the cause of their distress, and the necessity of a radical reform in the organic structure of society took possession of the public mind. But the manifold schemes for effecting this change, though containing some just views, abounded with theories the more seductive to popular imagination as they were vague and visionary. France, under the guidance of weak leaders, soon found herself divided into two hostile parties; the one allured by the bright promises of social regeneration, the other alarmed by the gloomy prospect of danger not less keenly felt for being exaggerated and undefined. Meanwhile the political factions, which had been overthrown by the revolution of 1848, taking courage from the distracted condition of the people, rallied, and forming a vast conspiracy against the republic, strove to re-establish their power on its ruins. They soon acquired the majority in the legislative assembly, plotted the expedition against Rome, and waged war against liberty at home.

When, in consequence of the prestige attached to his name, and the popularity of the views which he had put forth during his exile, Louis Napoleon was elected president, the spirit of the republic had long since died away. A profound diplomatist, eager for power, and a firm believer in his own destiny, Napoleon succeeded in gradually compromising his adversaries before the people, and in securing at the same time the support of the clergy and of the wealthy classes. Throwing the odium of all reactionary measures on the assembly, and assuming for himself the merit of all reforms he advocated order for the security of the higher classes, and plans for the improvement of the lower ones. So, step by step he stealthily advanced, till, seizing and casting aside the conspirators, he grasped in his own hands the destiny of the nation. It is not within our province to consider the moral aspect of the coup d'état; but this much may be said, that the founders of other monarchies had neither the object of saving their countries from impending ruin, nor even the semblance of popular suffrage. Certainly it is to be regretted that Louis Napoleon, menaced by old and new factions, by approaching anarchy, and the open hereditary hostility of the European powers, was forced to seize with an iron grasp the helm of state, to veil the statue of liberty, and to assume the garb of a despot. But when France willingly accepts the new regime, hails her ruler as her redeemer, and cheerfully bestows upon him the insignia of imperial dignity, we, believers in the right of popular sovereignty, feel bound to recognize that right in the French people, and trust that the glories which they have achieved under the star of Napoleon III. will be crowned with that liberty, which he himself has declared is the summit of all national greatness.

The political condition of France has always reacted on other nations, and after the coup d'état despotism became more threatening toward Sardinia. News of that event had scarcely reached the capitals of Europe, before remonstrances from various governments were addressed to the court of Turin, urging the necessity of abolishing or curtailing the guaranties of liberty secured by the constitution. The cabinets of Vienna, Florence, and Naples went so far as to intrude their advice on the king, and to insist that Sardinian institutions should be brought into conformity with those of the other states; for despotism abhors all contact with liberty. Victor Emmanuel, however, refused to violate the constitution which he had sworn to maintain; he spurned the menaces of his would-be advisers, and stood by the rights of the people. Finding themselves baffled in their efforts to extend their baneful influence over the only free State of Italy, those despots appealed to Louis Napoleon, denounced Sardinia as the centre of revolutionary agitation, and besought his interference, as the rebels of the South are at this moment begging support from foreign powers. But as the machinations of the petty rulers of the peninsula failed to enlist France in their cause, nay, as they were soon after ignominiously expelled from their thrones, while Victor Emmanuel, faithful to his mission, received the crown of Italy, so we believe that the civilization of Europe will not now be prostituted to the service of barbarism in America, and that the time is near at hand when the glorious banner, the emblem of the hopes of humanity, so lately trampled under the feet of parricides, shall again proudly wave from the great lakes to the Gulf of Mexico.

The attacks of the Sardinian journals upon foreign sovereigns formed one of the principal grievances of which Austria complained; and although Cavour and Azeglio declined to restrict in any way the freedom of the press, they admitted the necessity of making some provision to bring the offenders before the courts in cases of libel. For this purpose the administration introduced a bill, which, being apparently an act of submission to foreign governments, was met with vigorous opposition by the liberal party. The conservatives, on the contrary, not only supported it, but took the occasion of this discussion to expatiate on the excesses of the press, and to demand more severe restrictions. Cavour, perceiving that this party would force the government into reactionary measures, at once abandoned it, and threw himself into the ranks of those liberals who acknowledged Urbano Rattazzi as their leader. This statesman had acquired a prominent position in the house; he had been a member of the cabinet presided over by Gioberti, had succeeded him on his resignation, had declared war against Austria, and had retired on the defeat of Novara. From that time he began to advocate a more moderate policy, in accordance with the exigencies of the times, and, although he opposed the bill under discussion, he tendered his support to the ministry on condition that certain reforms should be energetically carried out. Cavour, on his own responsibility, and in opposition to the majority of the cabinet, boldly accepted his offer, and with him and his friends formed a third party, of which he became the chief. Thus these two patriots, starting from opposite points, met each other, and in a peaceful fusion they accomplished the union of the conservative and the progressive forces of the nation. By this means Cavour acquired the control of more vital elements, the advantage of Rattazzi's juridical science, his administrative talent, his keen dialectic power, his eloquence and popularity. His alliance, however, with a party which was regarded as opposed to the administration, was considered so imprudent that Azeglio felt bound to send instructions to the ministers abroad, directing them to allay the suspicions which it might have engendered at the foreign courts. But, although reproved by his colleagues and denounced as an apostate by those who look with aversion upon all progress and development, Cavour, nothing daunted, continued his course; and within three months he nominated his new ally to the speakership of the house, and carried the election. This was too much for the cabinet to bear; its dissolution followed, and Azeglio was appointed to form a new administration. Whereupon Cavour retired, confident that he would soon return to power with increased strength.

During the parliamentary recess Cavour again visited England and Scotland. While in London he made a midnight tour of inspection, under the guidance of a detective, through the lowest haunts of vice and crime in that metropolis, in order to make himself acquainted by personal observation with the actual condition of the lower classes. On his return to Paris he met Rattazzi by appointment, and the two statesmen had important interviews with the emperor, to whom they had the opportunity of representing the true condition of affairs in Sardinia, and of urging upon him the claims of Italy.

In the absence of Cavour, Azeglio, in order to propitiate the liberal party, introduced a bill for regulating civil marriage. Hitherto the law had considered marriage as a contract essentially united with the sacrament, and submitted it to ecclesiastical rule. Marriage was thus left under the control of the clergy, who became the only magistrates recognized for its celebration, the only judges in all matters relating to it, and the official guardians of the civil state. The evil consequences derived from this confusion of laws and offices could not be overlooked. Whatever were the religious opinions of the parties to be wedded, they were obliged to conform themselves to the regulations of the church. No marriage was permitted between parties of whom only one was properly baptized, or of whom one had previously taken orders, as if the State acknowledged some magic effect inherent to the imposition of hands by a bishop, which should forever disqualify the citizen from family duties and affections. The marriage between unbaptized people was valid; but if one chose to be baptized, the former tie was at once broken, and the husband or the wife thus baptized was entitled to abandon the other party, and to marry again. The impediments of the canon law having been multiplied for the purpose of multiplying dispensations, and thus of increasing the revenue of the church, the State in recognizing them had become a mercantile agent, and sold the rights of the people for the benefit of the court of Rome. Against these enormities public opinion had long since protested, and Azeglio now set at work to comply with its demands. But his proposed reform reclaimed only a part of the rights of the State, and thus, while it called forth the wrath of the clergy, it failed to reconcile the people.

Cavour, on his return to Turin, found the administration embarrassed by the opposition both of the liberal and reactionary parties, and involved in a harassing contest with the Papal See. Weak and vacillating when bold measures were required, and ready to compromise on matters which do not admit of compromise, Azeglio was now obliged to resign. Before doing so, however, he advised the king to intrust the government to

Cavour, as the only man able to cope with the difficulties of the situation. Victor Emmanuel accepted the advice, but, unwilling to come to an open rupture with the pope, he desired Cavour to make another attempt at conciliation. On these terms he declined the appointment, and after several ineffectual efforts on the part of the conservatives to reconstruct the cabinet, he was at length intrusted with the administration on his own conditions. He assumed the presidency of the council and the department of finance.

From this time to the period of his death, with the exception of a short interval, Cavour continued to hold the reins of government. He at once impressed a deeper character of nationality upon the foreign policy, and when Austria confiscated the property of those among the Italians of Lombardy and Venetia who had become citizens of Sardinia, he protested in a memorandum against such an outrageous measure, and finally obtained its repeal. In his domestic policy, too, he carried out still more energetically the reforms and public improvements already referred to. He showed himself more and more attached to the spirit of the constitution; and encountering a strong and systematic opposition in the senate on account of his liberal views, instead of introducing new and more friendly members into that assembly, as the government had the right to do, he preferred an appeal to the ballot-box, and the result afforded him a new triumph.

Cavour now called Rattazzi to the cabinet as minister of Grace and Justice, and thus perfected that alliance which he had before inaugurated. He caused at once a bill to be introduced for the suppression of various religious corporations and for the taxation of the property of the church, which till now had been exempt. Although this law by no means included all the reforms demanded by the time, it was a severe blow to the ecclesiastical party. If liberty was not restored by that act to the numerous misguided people who, seduced by the bigotry of the past regime, had in their youth sacrificed on the altar of superstition the inalienable birthright of their personality, at least others were prevented from falling into the same slavery. If all the institutions antagonistic to civil progress were not swept away, their number was at least diminished. If all the public wealth was not returned to the community, which, bequeathed for its general weal, was now used to its prejudice, at least a considerable portion of land was redeemed which before was enfeoffed to the church. If, finally, the successors of the fishermen were not reduced to the standard poverty of their teacher, provision was made for the relief of the rural clergy, who, although the most laborious and deserving, were left to starvation amidst the affluence of the bishops.

While this reform was under discussion before the parliament, the high clergy left no means untried to defeat its passage, and fate seemed to conspire with them. Just at this time, within a few days, Victor Emmanuel had seen the grave close over the remains of his mother, of his lovely young wife, and of his only brother, and the priests who had personal access to him, availing themselves of his despondency, represented these calamities as indications of divine wrath, and a just punishment for his opposition to the church. It was no wonder that at such a time these artful intimations should make some impression on the king, overwhelmed by these successive bereavements, and that for a moment he should yield. Urged by the warnings and the menaces of his ecclesiastical advisers, he desired the ministry to withdraw the bill, and to effect a compromise with the court of Rome. At this request Cavour and the cabinet at once resigned. The rejoicing of the church party at this triumph was equalled only by the general alarm. But while the clergy were striving to form a new administration, Azeglio, with that generosity and lofty patriotism which have distinguished his whole life, flew to rescue the country from the impending danger. He at once demanded an audience at the palace, which for the first time was refused. In a few hours he presented himself again, and was again refused. He then wrote a letter to the king, first given to the public in a late English work.

The letter, bearing the date of April 29th, 1855, is as follows:

"Sire—In Spain it was once prohibited under pain of death to touch the king. There was one whose robe caught fire; no one ventured to lay hands on him, and the king was burnt to death. But were I to risk my head or the total loss of your majesty's favor, I would think myself the most vile of men if in a moment like this I allowed your refusal to see me to deter me from addressing you. Sire, believe in your old and faithful servant, who in your service has had no other object than your good, your fame, and the welfare of the country. I say it with tears in my eyes, and kneeling at your feet: Do not proceed further in the road you have taken—there is yet time; return to your previous one. A cabal of friars has succeeded in one day in destroying the work of your reign, in agitating the country, in undermining the constitution, and in obscuring your name for honesty and truth. There is not a moment to be lost. No official announcement has as yet made it impossible for you to retract. It was said that the crown desired to take counsel on the subject; let the crown say that these counsels have shown the proposed conditions to be inadmissible. Let what is just past be considered as if it had never been, and affairs will resume their normal and constitutional current. Sardinia will suffer every thing except being put anew under the priestly yoke. Witness in Spain the result of the monkish intrigues to bring the queen to sign a disgraceful concordat. To what has it reduced her! Similar intrigues produced the downfall of James Stuart, of Charles X., and many others. Your majesty knows well that the things which I predicted have come to pass. Believe me; this is not a question of religion, but of interest. Amadeus II. disputed for thirty years with Rome, and conquered at the last. Be firm, and your majesty will likewise conquer. Do not be incensed against me. This act of mine is the act of an honest man, of a faithful subject, and of a true friend."*

Such were the words of Azeglio, and they were not written

* The Vicissitudes of Italy since the Congress of Vienna. By A. L. V. Gretton. London, 1859.

in vain. Cavour was again summoned, the cabinet restored, the idea of a compromise dismissed, and the bill which had been the occasion of this contest received the approval of the parliament and the signature of the king. Had Cavour yielded, had Azeglio failed to express less noble sentiments to his sovereign, Victor Emmanuel would not now wear the crown of Italy. Let the names of Cavour and Azeglio be engraved on that crown. They have saved the king; they have saved Italy.

Thus far the chief object of Cavour had been to transform the ancient regime into a strictly constitutional government, and to unite it to other countries by the silver thread of commerce; but now that the spirit of freedom had infused vitality into the State, his purposes expanded and his action took a wider scope. The Crimean war was the first event which opened the way to this more extended arena. Although the alliance of the two western powers of Europe originated in the necessity of checking the menacing preponderance of Russia in the east, Napoleon had another object in view, that of breaking the union of those governments which, by the treaty of Vienna, had dishonored France, and brought about the downfall of his dynasty. This alliance would add greatly to his authority among nations, would awake England to the danger of his enmity as well as to the advantages of his friendship, sever her connection with the Czar, whom it would chastise, and place Austria either within his power or that of Russia. On one hand she would be drawn into a war against Russia, on the other into a collision with England and France; or, remaining neutral, she would estrange herself from all. In any event Austria would lose her influence.

Cavour perceived at once the motives and bearings of the Anglo-French alliance; he saw that Sardinia had a paramount interest in excluding Russia from the Bosphorus and the Dardanelles, the keys of the Mediterranean, and that the time had come when the treaty of Vienna, the rock on which Italy had been wrecked, was about to be shivered into fragments. He saw that in the approaching contest the true position of the

State was that where it might dispute with Austria the benefits of the alliance should she join the western powers, or meet her on the field should she ally herself with Russia. While he saw that it was only through foreign alliances that the ultimate destiny of the nation could be accomplished, he felt also that Sardinia owed it to herself to redeem her military reputation, as yet obscured by the defeat of Novara.

With these views Cavour ardently advocated in the council and the parliament the policy of joining the alliance. But he was met with violent opposition. It was regarded as sheer madness to engage Sardinia in a war with a powerful empire, her armies not yet organized, her finances embarrassed, and Austria threatening her frontier. It was urged that Russia would never forget the unprovoked insult, and that whatever might be the result of the conflict, she would still have power to oppose all future attempts to secure Italian nationality, while on the other hand the allies would be indifferent if not hostile. But he was inflexible; the very arguments used against him became weapons in his hands, and, although assailed on all sides by friends and foes, he defended the proposed alliance with giant power, and succeeded in carrying the resolution. The treaty of alliance was signed, and an army greater than had even been stipulated was dispatched to the Crimea. It is unnecessary here to speak of the exploits of that army, which, led by the gallant Alfonso Lamarmora, called forth the admiration of the allies. The day when the Sardinian troops withstood the first shock of the enemy at the battle of Tchernaya, and so bravely contributed to his defeat, was the dawn of Italian independence. There in the far east, where once flourished the Italian colonies, Sardinia, by the side of the French and English armies, consecrated in the blood of her sons the right of leadership in the national cause, and won the recognition of that right from the allied powers.

After the fall of Sebastopol, Cavour accompanied the king on his visit to France and England. Everywhere received with marks of that regard secured to him by his high character and position, he availed himself of this opportunity to unite in closer ties of friendship the house of Savoy with the sovereigns of those countries, and to place before the representatives of public opinion the true aspect of affairs in Italy, as yet greatly misunderstood.

At the close of the war, Sardinia, notwithstanding the opposition of Austria, was admitted on a footing of equality with the other powers in the congress of Paris, and Cavour was delegated to represent the country in that assembly. His extraordinary diplomatic skill was never more conspicuous than on that occasion. Having established his position among the members of the congress, and conciliated those whom he wished to make friends, he induced the French and the English representatives to bring the Italian question before the congress, and, for the first time, the voice of Italy was heard in the councils of Europe. Without expressing his highest aspirations, or hinting at territorial changes which might create alarm, Cavour confined his remarks to the actual condition of Sardinia in her relations with the other Italian states. He maintained that, surrounded on all sides by Austrian troops, she was unable to develop her institutions and resources; that she was menaced alike by the despotism of the Italian princes and the revolutionary spirit which it engendered; that the military occupation of the duchies and the legations was in direct violation of the treaties which guaranteed their independence; and, pointing out particularly the wretched condition of the papal dominions, he appealed to the powers of Europe to put an end to abuses which were the shame of civilization and a permanent source of danger to the peace of the peninsula. Thus pleading the national cause from a conservative point of view, and within the limits of diplomatic form, the Italian statesman obtained a hearing in the congress, and secured the sympathy of France and England. Although the Austrian delegates opposed the introduction of that subject as foreign to the object of the meeting, the discussion was carried on; and, in order to fix the attention of those two powers, he addressed papers to Count Walewsky and to Lord Clarendon, in which he forcibly reasserted the claims of the nation.

Cavour soon after laid before the parliament the proceedings of the congress. He assured the chambers that, although the opposition of Austria had prevented the passage of any resolution in favor of Italy, the Italian cause had become a European question; he declared that although the Austrian and Sardinian delegates had separated without personal rancor, yet each felt that the policy of the two nations was farther than ever from approximating; and, pointing out the dangers of the situation, he appealed to the patriotism of the parliament to sustain the government in the events which might arise.

The course followed by Cavour in the congress of Paris was approved by the chambers, and received with patriotic enthusiasm by the country, which now hailed him as its destined deliverer. From all parts of the peninsula addresses were presented to him, and engravings, statuettes, and medals in his honor, were distributed over the land. On the very day of the entrance of Francis Joseph into Milan, the Milanese forwarded to the corporation of Turin a large contribution for the monument in memory of the Sardinians who had fallen in the Crimea. Italians all over the world united in the purchase of cannon for Alessandria, and soon that fortress, armed with guns bearing the names of New York, Boston, San Francisco, and other cities, frowned defiance on the Austrian frontier. Meanwhile the Sardinian press opened a more fierce broadside against Austria, and the numerous refugees who, since 1848, had found a home and position in Turin, began to look toward their native states with hope for their approaching deliverance. The government of Vienna, on the other hand, felt that a revolution was brooding, the more formidable because under the auspices of monarchical institutions. That an insignificant state which a few years since had been entirely under her control, and twice crushed beneath her iron heel, should dare to summon the Austrian empire before the bar of the civilized world, and to denounce it as the disturber of the public peace and the violator of those very treaties by which it held its dominions, was more than the proud house of Hapsburg could bear. A brisk interchange of diplomatic notes between Vienna and Turin followed, in which the pedantry and the dulness of Count Buol were ill-matched against the power and cutting irony of Cavour. At length the Austrian chargé was recalled, and one fine morning it was whispered among the Turinese that Cavour had left for Plombières.

This visit to Napoleon had been planned and brought about by Cavour himself; and it was on this occasion that the preliminaries of the alliance between France and Sardinia were settled, and the marriage of the Princess Clotilde with Prince Napoleon determined on, as the symbol and bond of the alliance. The Emperor's new year's greeting to Baron Hübner, which gave the first indication of the approaching storm, is yet fresh in our memory.

Whatever might have been at that time the opinion of Napoleon on the possibility of avoiding a conflict between Austria and Sardinia, it is certain that Cavour considered war as inevitable. The principles represented by the two countries were so opposed, and their estrangement was so complete, that from the first he saw that no compromise was possible, and that Italy must submit to Austrian rule, or be free, from the Alps to the Adriatic. He however adhered to the terms of mediation which England sent to Vienna, and afterward to the proposal of a congress made by Russia, simply to prove to Europe that Italy was disposed to maintain peace if by peace she could obtain satisfaction. Meanwhile he availed himself of the delay to allay the bitter feeling which the prospect of war had aroused in England, in Germany and in France, and to prepare for the coming crisis.

Victor Emmanuel, in his address to the parliament in the beginning of 1859, announced that the political horizon was not entirely serene. Professing himself not insensible to the cry of anguish which reached him from all parts of Italy, he pledged himself to march resolutely forward to meet the events of the future, "a future," said he, "which could not but be prosperous, since the policy of my government rests on justice, love of country and liberty, and on the sympathy which these ideas inspire." In the mean time Cavour, holding a kind of dictatorship under the king, was vigorously urging on preparations for war. He replenished the treasury, increased the army, strengthened the fortifications, reorganized the militia, and intrusted to Garibaldi the enlistment and command of the volunteers, who from all parts of the peninsula were flocking to the national standard; while in his foreign policy he strove to secure the friendship or at least the neutrality of the European governments, and to cast upon the court of Vienna, where it belonged, the responsibility of approaching hostilities. To the same end, on his return from Plombières, he had made a tour to Baden to visit the regent of Prussia, and had granted to Russia the privilege of making Villafranca a coal depôt and a harbor for her steamers; a concession which was intended both to gratify that power and to deal a blow to Austria, whose interests in the Mediterranean were thus counterbalanced by those of a rival empire.

The circumstances of the commencement of the war are well known. Cavour had given promise to England that he would abstain from any hostile demonstration toward Austria, and France had declared that she would aid Sardinia only in case of her being attacked. But while the preliminaries for a European congress were under discussion, Francis Joseph suddenly broke off all negotiations, and sent his ultimatum to Turin, requiring the government to disarm immediately, on penalty of an invasion. With this arrogant summons Cavour of course declined to comply. He immediately obtained a bill from the parliament vesting absolute authority in the king during the war, assumed the control of the war department, and placed the army in a defensive position. On the 29th of April, 1859, the Austrians crossed the Ticino, the French troops hastened across the Alps and the sea, and the trumpet of war echoed through Italy. The elements were against the enemy; the rains which had fallen in torrents had swollen the rivers and canals, and the floodgates and dykes, which divert the waters into the extensive rice-fields, having been removed by the inhabitants, the whole country was inundated, and the invaders were prevented from marching on the capital. They were soon driven from the territory, and within sixty days the victories of Magenta and Solferino brought the allied armies to the Mincio on their triumphant way toward the Adriatic.

In the midst of these splendid victories, the news of the interview at Villafranca fell like a thunderbolt upon Italy. To Cavour it was a crushing blow. He seemed to feel the concentrated bitterness of the nation. Only two days before, he had sent his greetings to his countrymen in America, and pledged his faith that the final triumph of the common cause was near at hand;* and now the object which had been for centuries the aspiration of patriots and martyrs, the aim of his hopes and labors, he saw vanish at the very moment when it appeared almost within his grasp. The cry of anguish which arose from the Italians fell upon his heart like a reproach, and the blood of those who had fallen on the plains of Lombardy cried to him from the ground. The very darkness in which he was left as to the motives of the peace of Villafranca, made him suspect that Italy, and he himself, had been betrayed. It is said that for a time he seemed to have lost his usual self-control; that he declined an interview requested by the emperor; that he urged the king to reject the terms of the peace, to recall his army, and to leave Napoleon to his designs. Whatever truth may be in these statements, it is certain that as soon as he heard of the sudden close of the war he resigned his office and retired to his country-seat at Leri. He retired to decline the responsibility of an act which he considered disastrous to his country, to keep aloof from all arrangements which would compromise the national movement, and as a private citizen to exert his influence over the people in that course of moral resistance which was to follow. Writing to a friend a few days after his retirement, he said: "This resolution of retiring from office has not

* See note A.

been dictated either by anger or discouragement. I have full faith in the triumph of the cause for which I have striven till now, and I am still ready to devote to it what little of life and power may yet be granted to me. But I am profoundly convinced that at this moment any participation in public affairs would be hurtful to my country. The destinies of Italy have been transferred to the hands of diplomacy. I am in bad odor with the diplomatic world; while my resignation is so acceptable that its effect will be to render diplomatists more favorably disposed toward unhappy central Italy, whose destinies they are about to decide on. There are circumstances in which a statesman cannot put himself too prominently forward. There are others in which the welfare of the very cause he serves requires him to retire from notice. This is the demand that the present condition of affairs makes upon me. A man of action, I retire from public life for the good of my country."

The policy of Cavour, both before and after the peace of Villafranca, cannot be fully understood without an inquiry into the causes which led Napoleon to engage in the Italian war, and to bring it to so sudden a close before its object was accomplished. That the alliance between him and Victor Emmanuel was due in a measure to his personal attachment to the cause of Italy, there can be no doubt. Descended from a family which traces its origin to Tuscany and Venice, and nearly allied to the great Corsican, he had been brought to Italy while yet a boy, and had found there a home in his exile. While his first impressions, his sympathies, and early associations, connected him closely to the country, his strong passions and will, his deep and tenacious nature, rendered him more an Italian than a Frenchman. In his youth he had belonged to the society of the Carbonari; he had taken a prominent part in the revolution of the Romagna, in which he had lost a brother; he had contracted many warm friendships, cemented by the perils and the romantic adventures incident to conspiracy. To this, if we add the numerous ties which bind the family of the Bonapartes to Italy, the ideas of the founder of the dynasty concerning her future destiny, preserved as a sacred tradition among his relatives, his grateful remembrance of the services and fidelity of the Italian soldiers in his wars with Spain and Russia, and his regrets, more than once expressed in his captivity, that he had done no more for that country, we may safely conclude that the third Napoleon had motives sufficient to avail himself of any opportunity consistent with his policy for promoting the interests of the Italian nation. His policy, happily, was entirely in unison with his feelings. Although by the Crimean war he had succeeded in breaking up the alliance of those powers which had guaranteed the execution of the treaty of Vienna, as far as it regarded territorial arrangements it still remained in force. His dynasty, however, would not be firmly established until Waterloo should be avenged by the complete blotting out of that treaty, and a war for Italian independence offered the readiest means for producing this result. To accomplish it by an attack in the direction of the Rhine or across the channel, would have brought upon him a European coalition. But by striking at Austria in the peninsula, he would reach the power which had most contributed to render that treaty offensive, and engage in a cause which would command the sympathy and admiration of the world. In any event he would be able to confine the struggle within the limits of that country, and thus avert the danger of a general war.

But there were other reasons which influenced Napoleon in espousing the Italian cause. While this was in accordance with his feelings and his dynastic interests, it coincided also with the traditional policy of France. France has not only been at all times the champion of civilization throughout the world, but has been always hostile to the domination of Austria over the peninsula. The geographical and ethnographical affinities which bind France to Italy, separate both from Austria. This antagonism appears throughout all French history, and forms one of its most salient characteristics. Whenever the French people have risen to the summit of power, one of their leading objects has been the reconstruction of Italy as a nation. To this end

Henry IV. directed his genius; and it is remarkable, that the first step he proposed toward its accomplishment was to extend the sway of the house of Savoy over the territory held by Austria. Had his designs been carried out, had not the dagger of Ravaillac cut short his career, Italy would have been probably an independent nation two centuries ago. This policy was not relinquished with the death of that great king; it was favored by Richelieu, and nearly accomplished by Louis XV. a century later. D'Argenson, the minister of that monarch, characterized by Voltaire as fit to be secretary of state in the republic of Plato, was an earnest advocate of this idea. There were then, as now, not wanting in France narrow-minded men, who regarded with jealousy the growth of a great nation beyond the Alps; and of such he thus writes: "They may quote as much as they please the saying of Cardinal d'Ossat about the young wolves of Savoy, and say that should the king of Sardinia become so powerful we would be obliged to fortify Lyons. These are but prejudices instigated by the hatred of Spain. There will be still in all cases a great difference of power between Sardinia and France. Our danger arises only from one source, the house of Austria. Neighbors we must have, and nothing better could happen to us than that the small states should grow at the expense of the large ones. . . . It would be glorious for France to break the chains of Italy, and to deliver her from the yoke of Germany. It would be a mortal blow to Austria, as it would restrict her power within her own limits. This would mark a great era in the history of France, and the king would gather from it a glory which would render his reign illustrious to all posterity."*

It is needless to say that this same idea directed the policy of the first Napoleon. But the conqueror of Marengo, in his efforts to introduce into Europe the principles of the French revolution, was obliged to disregard the rights of nationality.

* See the Memoires du Marquis d'Argenson, tom. iii. For the documents relative to the traditional policy of France in regard to Italy, see the work of Canestrini; Della Politica Piemontese nel Secolo xvii.

His course being opposed by the potentates of Europe, he was forced into conquest to give expansion to the civilizing influences of France, and to defend her territory from threatened invasion. Italy thus fell under his power. But that his dominion over the peninsula had but a temporary character, and that it was intended to prepare it for its own independence, he himself declared, not only at St. Helena, but as early as 1805, when addressing the Italian deputation charged with offering him the crown of Italy, he said: "My intention has always been to render the Italian nation free and independent. I accept the crown, and will preserve it, but only for such time as my own interests may require." The predominant idea of Napoleon I. was to secure the preponderance of France in the councils of Europe, under the ascendency of the Bonaparte dynasty, and it continues to be that of the present emperor. But while the former strove to enforce this policy by gigantic wars and conquests more in accordance with his own tendencies and the age, his successor proposes to accomplish the same end by moral rather than by physical force. Educated in a more refined civilization, with a character formed in exile and misfortune, prone to trace political events to their general causes, thoroughly imbued with the views of his predecessor, yet fully aware of their shortcomings, he seeks the same result through means more in conformity with the present time. Conquest would be to him more ruinous than it was to his great relative. The spirit of nationality so characteristic of our day, aided by the predominance of material interests, and the jealousies and memories of the past, would render such a course utterly disastrous. In proof of this we may quote his own words, addressed to the Italians in one of his proclamations during the late war: "Your enemies," said he, "who are also mine, would diminish the universal sympathy which Europe feels for your cause, by attempting to make people believe that I make war only for my personal ambition, or for the aggrandizement of the territory of France. If there are men who do not understand their age, I am not of that number. In the present enlightened condition, one is far greater for the moral influence which he is able to exert than for fruitless conquests. It is this moral influence that I seek with pride, by contributing to render free one of the most beautiful countries of Europe."

The central idea of his policy could not be more clearly and forcibly expressed. The first step in its development is to secure the political existence and power of the Latin races, by uniting them in a confederation headed by France, and eventually to be augmented by others belonging to the Sclavonic and Germanic groups. He seeks not the preponderance of France by chaining other nations to her car, as the first Napoleon attempted to do, but by creating such circumstances in the European policy as to induce them to follow her course. By thus securing allies instead of rivals, he would be aided in carrying out his designs for the advancement of civilization throughout the world, and in actualizing his early definition of the empire: "L'empire c'est la paix." It was in this point of view that he formed the alliance with England, and courted the support not only of Sardinia, but of Naples, Spain and Sweden; that he exerted his influence for the national unity and independence of the Danubian principalities, favored the plans of Spain in Morocco and Mexico, and proposed her admission among the great powers; that he promoted the opening of the isthmus of Suez, in order to give back to the nations situated on the Mediterranean their commercial preponderance; that he joined England in the war against China, undertook the expedition to Syria, and finally engaged in the cause of Italy, and both in war and in peace made himself the patron of her nationality.

The expedition against Rome, which seemed entirely opposed to this object, was in fact a step toward its accomplishment. Although that event took place under the presidency of Louis Napoleon, it had been matured by the preceding administration, and was forced upon him by the legislative assembly. In accepting that measure he obtained the support of the clergy and other reactionary parties, consolidated his power, gained a foothold in the very heart of the peninsula, counterbalanced the influence of Austria, kept open the Italian question, and forced the pope to assume his true position of an antagonist to modern civilization. The development of this profound policy was necessarily gradual, and little calculated to inspire confidence in the less thoughtful among the Italians, to whom the emperor appeared as the accomplice of Austria, the upholder of the abuses of the papal government, and a treacherous and formidable enemy. The bombs of Orsini warned him that the time had come for more decided action; that although longer delay might contribute to his security at home, it was attended with peril from abroad. But he proved on that occasion a true friend to Italy, and even conveyed the assurance of his friendship to the misguided enthusiast who had so wantonly sought his life. The letter which Orsini wrote on the eve of his execution, in which he pointed out Napoleon III. as the coming liberator of Italy, was allowed to be read at his trial and to be published throughout the peninsula.

The motives which led Napoleon to espouse the cause of Italy explain the policy of Cavour in securing his alliance. We may now inquire into the causes of the peace of Villafranca. It must be borne in mind that the object of the alliance between France and Sardinia was the expulsion of Austria from Lombardy and Venetia, and the consequent aggregation of those provinces to the dominions of Victor Emmanuel, as the first step toward the reorganization of the country. But as the war progressed a new element was developed, of whose existence Cavour had long been aware, but which Napoleon had not fully counted upon. This was the growing tendency of the other Italian States toward unification. This tendency had early so far manifested itself as to group the municipalities into states, but from various causes its progress had been arrested, and, crystallizing around several centres, the nation up to this time had remained divided. In 1848 Cavour, as we have seen, had accepted the idea of a confederacy as the only policy which seemed practicable, and the one best calculated to effect the ultimate consolidation of Italy. It was fortunate, however, that the project failed; for while in the United States such a form of government is a necessity, from its vast extent of territory, its varied interests, and irresistible force of expansion, in Italy it would be undesirable from her limited area, equal only to that of the States of New York and Pennsylvania, her common civilization, and her facility of intercommunication. A confederacy among the Italian monarchies, and no other would be possible at present, by multiplying dynastic interests would create new antagonisms; and thus the complications and the dangers inherent to federal institutions would be vastly increased. Add to this that the States as they existed before the late war were but artificial and incomplete aggregations of parts of the nation, without life or history of their own, and that the cities, the only great individualities of the country, could not properly be subjected to any other organization than to the government which represents Italy herself.

In the civilization of the present day great states alone can compete with the more advanced nations; and the Italian people, receiving a new impulse from the free institutions of Sardinia, now rapidly converged toward their political unity. The Austrian troops had not yet crossed the Ticino before the central States, abandoned by their rulers, hastened to place themselves under her protection, and Cavour was not backward in granting it. He sent commissioners to those States, organized new governments in the name of Victor Emmanuel, abolished the custom-houses, promulgated the Sardinian laws, and prepared the country for that union which he could not as yet effect in an official capacity. In this work he was aided by the enlightened co-operation of many patriots, and particularly of Baron Ricasoli in Florence, to whom, next to Cavour and Garibaldi, Italy is indebted for the conquest of her nationality. Descended from one of the most ancient families of Tuscany, endowed with a refined and cultivated intellect, a stern integrity and an indomitable will, and exercising a commanding influence over his countrymen, Ricasoli was chiefly instrumental in leading Tuscany forth to lay on the altar of patriotism her traditional glories, and to merge her individual life into that of the nation. While these aupicious circumstances gave promise that before the close of the war a great part of the country would be consolidated into one free government, the world was startled by the sudden news of the peace of Villafranca.

For this step on the part of Napoleon various causes have been assigned, prominent among which was his supposed desire to check this unexpected movement of annexation. But events have proved that his real object was to perfect rather than to prevent it. The emperor could not oppose the acceptance by Victor Emmanuel of the crown of Italy without violating the principle on which he held his own; and on entering Milan, while exhorting the Italians to fly to the national standard, he had formerly pledged himself not to interfere with the wishes of the people in regard to their future organization. Perceiving now that a confederation would not be accepted by the States, and knowing that their union would enable them to achieve their independence by their own exertions, he had the courage to cut short the war in his brilliant career of victory, and to leave them to accomplish their own destiny. The continuance of the war might free Venice from Austrian rule; but it would at the same time, in the new issue which had arisen, involve him in a direct conflict with the pope, whose possessions had been already encroached upon, a conflict which would endanger his security at home from the intrigues of the clergy, and other parties who, though indifferent or hostile to the interests of the church, would gladly avail themselves of this pretext to plot against his throne. He could not take part in a direct struggle for Italian unity without openly violating international law, which still protected the Italian princes, thus incurring the danger of a coalition. Such a course, too, would excite the opposition of certain classes in France, who, although sympathizing with the freedom of Italy, regarded with jealousy the prospect of her consolidation and increasing power.* Add to this, that in view of the possibility of a long resistance on

* See note B.

the part of the enemy intrenched in the fortresses, the emperor had early entered into a conditional alliance with Kossuth and other popular leaders, for the purpose of promoting, in case of necessity, revolutionary movements in Hungary and other disaffected portions of the Austrian empire. A continuance of the war would thus greatly widen its sphere and complicate its results; and when it became apparent that its object could be accomplished by leaving the Italians to gain strength by consolidation, it was obviously the wisest policy to avoid the impending dangers of coalition and revolution, by withdrawing from the field at a moment when he found himself in a position to dictate the condition certain to produce that result, the non-intervention of Austria.

Although the chief object of the peace of Villafranca was the independence of Italy, to be won by the Italians themselves, it secured other scarcely less important ends. The problem which Napoleon III. seems to have proposed to himself was to obtain the maximum of results by the minimum of war. By the sudden termination of the campaign, while he saved himself from the risk of losing what he had gained, he prevented at once the alliance on the eve of being consummated between Austria and Prussia, and arrested the march of the Prussian troops across the Rhine; he made his power felt by the governments of Europe, whose interference he openly disregarded in his new territorial arrangements; and having checked the pride of Austria, he won her friendship by his magnanimity, when, disheartened by a series of defeats, she saw herself at once saved from destruction with a comparatively small sacrifice.

On his return from the Italian campaign, Napoleon himself declared, in his address to the Corps d'État, that although he found Europe in arms ready to dispute his successes or to aggravate his disasters, he would have still continued the war if the means to be employed had not been disproportioned to the intended result; that prosecuting the struggle on the Adige, he would have been obliged to accept the challenge on the Rhine, strengthen himself by an alliance with revolution, and risk what a sovereign should never do except for the independence of his own country; and pleading the interests of France as the cause which had induced him to put an end to the war, he closed his address with the following words: "The peace which I have concluded, as every day will reveal, will be fruitful in good results for the happiness of Italy, the influence of France, and the quiet of Europe." Looking now to Italy, united from Susa to Syracuse, a union perfected within less than two years from that time, we see the glorious fulfilment of those prophetic words; and the peace, which seemed a mortal blow to the dawning hope of the Italians, by the stipulation at first withheld from public knowledge, that no coercion would be employed to enforce its offensive terms, inaugurated in Italy the great principle of popular sovereignty, and became the keystone of the Italian nationality.

We have seen that Cavour, on withdrawing from the cabinet after the peace of Villafranca, retired to his estate at Leri. But he still remained the recognized head of the national movement; and his opposition to that act before its full significance was disclosed, added to his popularity. He was not long, however, in discovering the thread of the apparently tortuous policy of the emperor, and he eagerly availed himself of it. From his retreat he kept up a constant correspondence with the leaders of central Italy, urging them to be firm and uncompromising. The administration of Rattazzi, who had succeeded him, trammelled by embarrassments of all kinds, looked to Leri for counsel and direction; and the people of the Tuscan and Æmilian provinces, encouraged by his example and strengthened by his advice, positively refused to receive back their princes, notwithstanding the urgent entreaties of the emperor, and declined to adhere to any plan of adjustment but that of annexation to Sardinia. At this crisis Cavour was recalled to the cabinet; and reassuming the presidency of the council and the department of foreign affairs, he at once dissolved the chamber elected after the union of Lombardy, caused central Italy to be divided into electoral districts, and declared to the powers of Europe that the restoration of the dukes being utterly impossible, and any other arrangement of the organization of those provinces fraught with danger, he felt it his duty to accept on behalf of the king their union with Sardinia. Napoleon had meantime offered new propositions to Sardinia, which, although less offensive than those of the late treaty, were yet opposed to the absolute annexation of Tuscany and the Romagna. But Cavour at once declined them; and proposed instead, to submit that question, which had been already decided by the legislatures of those States, to the direct vote of the people—thus appealing to the same source which the emperor recognized as the origin of his own power, and to which he had just proposed to refer the annexation of Savoy and Nice to France.

The union of these provinces had been agreed upon at the interview of Plombières, as a condition of the alliance which was to deliver Lombardy and Venetia from the Austrian yoke. France had long before claimed the possession of Savoy and Nice, and had always enforced this claim whenever a favorable occasion presented itself. Nice, a part of ancient Provence, seemed rather allied to the French than to the Italian nation; and Savoy, in geographical position, language, and interests, was in fact but a French province. They had been wrested from France by the treaty of Vienna, and Napoleon was now led to request their surrender not only by dynastic exigencies, but also by the necessity of affording compensation to the French people for the sacrifice of blood and treasure which the war would entail on them. The peace of Villafranca having left a part of the Italian territory in the possession of Austria, Napoleon for the time waived his claim; but now, as the annexation was rapidly progressing, and Sardinia expanding, he desired that that stipulation should be complied with. Cavour could not refuse, consistently with his principles and the welfare of his country, inasmuch as in subjecting the cession to the vote of the people, the right of popular sovereignty would be maintained, and a precedent established which would be highly advantageous to the settlement of similar questions which might arise in the peninsula. The inhabitants of Savoy and Nice were therefore summoned to the ballot-box to decide whether they would belong to France or to Italy. An overwhelming majority being in favor of French rule, those provinces passed under the dominion of the empire, while Parma, Modena, Tuscany, and the Legations, by the voice of their people, hailed the young chief of the ancient house of Savoy as king of Italy.

Such was the first great achievement toward Italian unity, which early in 1860, had been attained chiefly through the wise policy of Cavour. Well might the king, in addressing the new parliament, congratulate the country that "Italy was no longer the Italy of municipal governments or that of the middle ages, but the Italy of the Italians." Attended by his minister, he departs to visit the new dominions which not the sword of the conqueror but the hearts of the people had bestowed upon him. The enthusiasm with which the illustrious visitors are received in the new provinces exceeds all description. Now for the first time the sentiment which before had been so long restrained by the boundaries of cities and states, overleaps all barriers, and is merged in the deep emotion of patriotism; all traces of ancient feuds have vanished; the once rival cities emulate each other in their expressions of mutual affection. Genoa returns to Pisa the chains of her harbor seized centuries before, and to this time held by that city as a trophy; the sword which Castruccio Castracane, the Ghibelline chieftain, had in the 14th century bequeathed to him who should deliver the country, is now conferred upon Victor Emmanuel; and the venerable Niccolini, the national poet, in whose patriotic strains the fire of Dante still burns, hastens with tottering steps to present to the king his master-piece, "the Arnaldo da Brescia," blessing "the kind fate that had allowed him, before his eyes close on the sweet air of Italy, to see the aspiration of his life accomplished." Let Parma and Modena, Florence and Bologna, deck themselves in their splendid array, to welcome the warrior and the statesman who have given to them national life; let the people tender to them the triumphs which Rome bestowed upon her conquerors; let the arts revive their ancient glory and lay their tributes at their feet; let music, painting, and poetry celebrate the union of central Italy with Sardinia. It is the dawn of the nation's birthday.

But another act of the great drama now opens; another hero now appears on the stage. We search in vain the archives of history for heroic deeds and marvellous achievements like those which a little more than a year ago sent a thrill of admiration and joy through the hearts of all the friends of liberty in both hemispheres. For this we must go back to the legendary ages, when the gods mingled with men, the ages of Hercules and Theseus, of Odin and Thor; and when centuries shall have passed away, and Italy shall again have reached the apex of her greatness, and the memory of the great chieftain shall have been still more embellished by popular imagination, the name of Garibaldi will be invested with mythical glory surpassing that of the Cid in Spain and Jeanne d'Arc in France. On the 11th of May, 1860, Garibaldi, at the head of one thousand patriots, landed at Marsala. He came, he saw, he conquered. Within less than four months he had delivered ten millions of Italians from the hated yoke of the Bourbons.

For a work like that which Garibaldi accomplished Cavour had no power. A statesman far removed from revolutionary impulses, his genius consisted rather in directing events than forcing them. Believing in the ultimate union of the nation, his original plan had been the consolidation of northern Italy into one kingdom, which should gradually absorb the entire peninsula. But the peace of Villafranca having defeated that design, his next object became the annexation of central Italy. The instinct of the people, however, outstripped this process of gradual absorption, and hastened to precipitate an immediate union of the whole country. Of this instinct Garibaldi was the great representative. Essentially a man of the masses, sharing their virtues as well as their faults, with the heart of a lion in the frame of an athlete; trained amidst the tempests of the ocean, and on the battle-fields of the old and new worlds; and burning with the fire of liberty and patriotism, the hero of Caprera became the leader of the national movement at the moment when it began to assume a more revolutionary character.

This brings us to the most embarrassing period of the political career of Cavour. On one hand it was impossible for Sardinia openly to take part in the expeditions of Garibaldi directed against the king of the Two Sicilies, still on his throne, and holding with her neutral if not friendly relations. Such a step would probably have induced Austria again to take the field, and in the face of such a flagrant violation of international law, France would have been unable to protect the country from an armed intervention. On the other hand that movement could not be prevented without seriously endangering the national cause. The idea of political unity had taken such deep hold on the public mind, that any attempt to check its development would have resulted in revolution. Again, the court of Rome was gathering the scum of Europe to its support; and having secured the services of General Lamoricière, it threatened the new kingdom with an alliance with Francis II., openly supported by Austria and other powers. In this emergency Garibaldi appeared, and organized his expeditions for the deliverance of southern Italy. Although his success might be doubtful, his bold attempt would spread terror among the enemy, divide the forces of Naples and Rome, and drive them from their threatening attitude. So, without either encouraging or preventing the departure of Garibaldi, Cavour awaited the events, ready to avail himself of all the advantages which might result from the daring enterprise, or to avert any danger which it might provoke. This policy evinced scarcely less boldness than the achievements of the dashing leader himself. The principle of national rights over dynastic interests was regarded as so heretical by the cabinets of Europe, that it was only due to the skill of Cavour that their opposition was confined to protest. By appealing to their conservative tendencies, and by representing that an effort to put down the movement by force of arms would cause a revolution throughout the peninsula, and endanger the existence of monarchical institutions, he saved the expeditions from an armed intervention. But when success appeared certain, Cavour changed his policy of inaction for a course of active sympathy, and not only allowed volunteers to depart from the ports of the State and subscriptions for their aid to be widely circulated, but he himself afforded the enterprise direct assistance.

Before the war of 1859, Sardinia had proposed an alliance with the king of Naples on condition of his granting a constitution to his people and joining in the war against Austria. Hitherto he had resisted all advances. But now that Garibaldi, having possessed himself of Sicily, was knocking at the gates of Naples, Francis II. hastened to accede to those terms, and proposed to share with Sardinia the pontifical dominions. But it was too late. Since the war had commenced, such changes had occurred in the peninsula that Cavour in turn declined the proposed alliance; and as England, France, and Russia urged upon him its acceptance, he wisely insisted on delaying all negotiations on the subject until that sovereign should prove himself able to maintain his throne; and in the mean time claimed as a preliminary that he should recognize the independence of Sicily. But Garibaldi left no time for decision; he at once made his triumphant entry into Naples, while the fugitive king took refuge in Gaeta.

Between Cavour and Garibaldi there existed great differences of character. The one was endowed with comprehensive genius, with a clear, keen intellect, that neither imagination nor impulse could seduce; affluent, aristocratic, reserved, often satirical and imperious, unyielding in his opinions, with power to bend the convictions of others to his own; too confident in himself to court popular favor, and devoted to labors more calculated to excite the admiration of the thoughtful than to dazzle the multitude. The other, of more limited capacity, but of wider sympathies, was ruled by imagination and impulse, disposed to regard all questions from a single point of view, democratic by birth and principles, of Spartan simplicity of life and manners, despising rank and wealth, kind, straightforward, easily influenced by all who approached him in the name of patriotism, and from his wonderful success as well as from his rare personal qualities, the idol of the masses. Both true patriots, both equally courageous and energetic, while the one exerted his genius in diplomatic strategy, the other was engaged in irregular warfare. Both equally ambitious to serve their country, while one accepted the honors bestowed upon him, the other disdained all distinctions, but delighted to appear in public in his worn red shirt. Both of sterling integrity, while the one on entering office disposed of his shares in the public stocks to place himself beyond the reach of suspicion, the other during his dictatorship received but two dollars a day from the public treasury, and after conquering a kingdom, retired, like Cincinnatus of old, to his farm, to live by the labor of his hands.

These characteristics, combined with an intense hatred of all diplomacy, produced in Garibaldi a personal antipathy to Cavour, which, on the surrender of Nice culminated in open hostility. That his birthplace should have been ceded to Napoleon, whom he disliked still more than Cavour, he regarded almost as a personal insult; and although that surrender had been approved by the parliament and the king, and voted for by the people, Cavour appeared to him as its sole author. He did not see that had Nice been refused, the Italian cause would have been endangered, and that the minister who should have incurred the responsibility of the refusal would have been liable to impeachment as a traitor. He overlooked the fact that his expeditions had found a supporter in Cavour, who had protected them from foreign intervention, and that it was in no small degree due to his efforts that he was enabled to enter Naples alone, and to be received with open arms by the Neapolitan troops, who still held possession of the city. His prejudice, no doubt, was in a great measure the effect of the influences by which he was surrounded. He had, early in life, been connected with Mazzini, and long continued to manifest his sympathy with the republican party. But when Manin the Venetian patriot, urged the union of all parties under the leadership of the house of Savoy, he renounced his former alliance, and generously gave his adherence to the constitutional monarchy of Victor Emmanuel. Later, on becoming personally acquainted with the king, he found in his character, simplicity, straightforwardness, and patriotism, much that was congenial to himself, and he conceived for him a loyal attachment. This course was at the time bitterly condemned by his former associates, and by Mazzini himself. But now, in the hour of his triumph, those who not long before had been engaged in vilifying his name in Europe and in America, flocked to Naples, insinuated themselves again into his confidence, and by playing on his real or fancied grievances strove to widen the breach between him and Cavour, whom they justly regarded as the great supporter of constitutional monarchy, and the staunch opponent of their schemes. Good, unsophisticated, generous, and new in the art of government, the hero of the battle-field became a child in the hands of those adventurers; Naples, and Sicily fell under their control, and exhibited more completely than ever the effects of that disorganization to which they had been previously reduced by a long reign of despotism. From Gaeta, Francis II. now threatened an invasion of his former dominions, while Austria, from Verona and Mantua, and Lamoricière from Ancona, were preparing to act in concert with him. In this state of things it was necessary that southern Italy should at once declare her union with the northern and central provinces, and thus justify the intervention of Sardinia, by which alone regularity could be introduced into the administration, and the invasion resisted. The great majority demanded annexation; but Garibaldi, who had taken possession of the kingdom in the name of Victor Emmanuel, seemed to waver between his former adherence to Mazzini and his fidelity to the king. Pressed by public opinion to consult the vote of the people, he at last consented to open the ballot-box, but only on condition of the dismissal of Cavour from the cabinet. Such a request, destructive of all constitutional liberty, found no favor with the king; and Cavour, receiving new assurances of confidence from the parliament, decided on a bold movement. The situation was growing every day more alarming; while anarchy threatened Naples, the mercenaries of the pope were pouring in from all quarters, and Garibaldi himself was held in check on the Volturno, the republicans began to speak openly of attacking the French garrison at Rome and the Austrians in their fortresses. Baffled in their plan of removing Cavour from the government, they prevailed on Garibaldi to subordinate the annexation of southern Italy to the deliverance of Rome and Venice, and he, in fact, proclaimed that he would allow the union to be consummated only when he could crown Victor Emmanuel king of Italy on the Quirinal.

Cavour saw that the attempt to carry out this plan would bring certain defeat, involve Sardinia in a war with Austria, break up the French alliance, cause the abandonment of the non-intervention policy, and probably sacrifice the conquests already achieved. Had Garibaldi been able to carry out his dream, to make his triumphal passage across Umbria and the Marches, rout the troops of Lamoricière, put to flight the French army, expel Austria and bring aid to Hungary and Poland, his very successes would have provoked an armed intervention. His triumphs as well as his defeats appeared equally fatal to Italy. There was no time to lose; "If we do not reach the Cattolica before Garibaldi, we are lost," said Cavour to a friend. By a master-stroke of policy, he determined at once to take possession of Umbria and the Marches, push forward the army to Naples and Sicily, and to wrest from Garibaldi the leadership of the nation. The deputations from those provinces demanding immedate annexation, were at once favorably listened to, Cardinal Antonelli was summoned, in the name of Italy, to disband his mercenaries, the Sardinian army crossed the frontier, and the fleet set sail for the Adriatic. We need not here describe the victory of Castelfilardo and the siege of Ancona, when the papal army was scattered to the winds, Lamoricière taken prisoner, Perugia avenged, and the national flag unfurled over the papal dominions. Victor Emmanuel, at the head of his troops, now entered the Neapolitan territory, and, on approaching the camp at Capua, was met by Garibaldi, who, amidst the enthusiastic cheers of the two armies, saluted him king of Italy.

The wisdom of the policy followed by Cavour on this occasion can only be questioned by those who make the principle of nationality subservient to the interests of dynasties and to the claims of despotism. By taking possession of Umbria and the Marches and by occupying southern Italy, he defeated the rash designs of the republicans, and put an end to the not less menacing projects of Lamoricière and Francis II. He showed also a just appreciation of the character of Garibaldi, on whose patriotism, loyalty, and generous instincts, he confidently relied; and he was not mistaken; for scarcely had the king announced his intention to proceed to Naples, when the great chieftain, listening now to the voice of his heart, at once summoned the people to the ballot-box, and the annexation being voted for by a large majority, he at once resigned his dictatorship and retired to his humble home.

In reviewing the events of 1860 in southern Italy, if we were unacquainted with the actual sentiments of Garibaldi toward Cavour and his aversion to all diplomatic artifice, we might suspect that he had purposely allowed the irregularities of his administration, and menaced Rome and Venice for the sole object of alarming the European powers, and thus, of paving the way for subsequent events. As it was, it is due to Cavour that great impediments were turned into powerful means, and that the unity of Italy was secured by the coöperation of his friends as well as by the opposition of his foes.

On the 18th of February, 1861, the first Italian parliament representing united Italy convened in the old capital of Sardinia. The roar of the cannon which celebrates its first meeting mingles with that which announces the fall of Gaeta; the sound echoes throughout the peninsula, and bears to Austria and the papacy a warning of their approaching downfall. Italy at last revives; she revives in the unity of her people, her constitution and monarchy. She rises from beneath the ruins of the thrones which crushed her, the barriers which divided her, and takes her place among nations. Her standard proudly waves from Milan to Palermo; her army marches in triumph from Monte Rosa to the Ætna; her navy rides joyfully on the Mediterranean and the Adriatic. Now, for the first time, the countrymen of Alfieri and Parini take their seats by the side of those of Vico and Tasso; the countrymen of Ariosto and Volta with those of Dante and Galileo. But, alas! we look in vain in the parliament of the nation for the representatives of Venice and Rome. The lion of St. Mark is still chained to the throne of the Hapsburgs; the keys of St. Peter, the emblem of the thraldom of Italy, still hang on the walls of the Vatican.

The deliverance of these noble provinces now became the chief object of Cavour. He was not, however, permitted to carry out his grand designs. He led the people forth from their captivity to a height from whence the promised land lay stretched out before their gaze; but, like the prophet of old, he fell at the very entrance, bequeathing to his successors the glory of completing his great work. The principles by which this was to be accomplished, Cavour himself laid down, in one of his later and more comprehensive efforts, before the parliament now assembled.

Venice, the illustrious martyr, which had been sacrificed by the peace of Villafranca for the sake of the whole nation, must be rescued, he urged, either by purchase or conquest; the country speedily organized and strengthened in its military resources and alliances; and as an immediate war for the conquest was impossible, from the want of preparation at home, and the state of public sentiment abroad, he advocated the necessity of producing a change in this respect, by proving to the world the ability of the Italians to form a united, strong, and independent nation, based on the unanimous consent of the people, and to accomplish by themselves that great enterprise. Italy might thus effect the deliverance both of Venice and Rome whenever the favorable moment should arrive.

Rome, the immortal city which has for so many centuries concentrated in herself the history of all Italy, for her glories, magnificence and position, is the natural capital of the kingdom. The other cities, jealous of supremacy among themselves, yield precedence to her which they acknowledge as the head of the country, the symbol, the centre, and the complement of Italian unity, but which as a papal city inevitably becomes the antagonist of the national spirit and the stumbling-block of national liberty. When, therefore, the union had been sanctioned by the vote of the two houses, and measures introduced for its consummation, the parliament at once proclaimed Rome the seat of government, and urged the administration to enforce this claim. This resolution was brought forward by the advice of Cavour; and the speeches which he delivered on that occasion, among the last of his parliamentary career, were characterized by a peculiar clearness and force of language, breadth of thought, and earnestness of purpose. Dwelling on the necessity of uniting Rome to the nation, and thus of restoring that glorious city to civilization, in the name of Turin, to which he was attached by interest and affection, he declared that the present capital, which for the last thirteen years had nobly borne the burden of the national struggle, was ready to submit to this last great sacrifice, and for the sake of Italy cheerfully to waive her claims in behalf of the ancient city of the Cæsars.

Since, then, national right demanded the possession of Rome, it remains to be seen how Cavour proposed to effect it. He beheld enthroned in the Vatican the successor of an unbroken line of pontiffs reaching far back almost to the dawn of Christianity; the priest-king who holds a double sceptre in the name of the Almighty, and represents an institution which, though tottering and crumbling under the weight of many centuries, is sustained by a vast hierarchy, by time-honored maxims, by religious aspiration and saintly abnegation, as well as by superstition, party spirit, and political intrigue. He saw the papal throne, detested by the Italian people, under the protection of France, to whose alliance their late conquests were chiefly due. To abandon Rome to the church was to sacrifice the rights of the nation; to take possession of that capital was to incur the opposition of Napoleon, who declared that he would withdraw his troops only when the independence of the pope should be established. To secure this independence, Cavour now proposed to introduce into Italy the principle of a free church in a free state; a measure which, while it would restrict the pope to the exercise of his legitimate power, would deprive him of his political pretensions, restore Rome to the nation, and give freedom both to the church and the people. In this proposal Cavour aimed rather at political than at social results. But the issue involved in his reform is subordinate to high principles of social philosophy, and it is only by examining it in relation to those principles that the significance of his formula may be fully understood. The recognition of a free church in a free state not only implies the overthrow of the temporal power of the papacy, but is a direct denial of its spiritual sovereignty, which is the antithesis of the intellectual and religious freedom embodied in that reform, and which is the distinguishing characteristic of modern society. A passing glance at the origin and historic development of the papal institution will indicate its true position in reference to modern civilization, and the conditions under which that reform may be carried out.

The social mission of Christianity was to unite the race not by conquest, but by moral agencies calculated to bring mankind within the pale of a higher civilization; and for this end it was necessary that the Christian system should maintain that unity which is the basis of all scientific theories as well as of religious institutions. But its internal unity being early impaired by the introduction of new elements freely borrowed from pagan symbolism and judaic legends, and by the springing up of numerous heresies, Christianity gradually expanded into an outward organization, which assumed, in addition to its religious prerogatives, legislative and political functions. At first democratic, then aristocratic, it finally culminated in a monarchy with the Bishop of Rome at its head, who was soon recognized as the spiritual king of Christendom, the divinely appointed interpreter of the Christian faith, the centre and the symbol of religious unity. This transformation took place in an age when religion controlled all individual and social life; when theology was the synthesis of all science, canon law the only existing code, and the church the only spiritual agency. The pope thus came to be regarded as the exponent of civilization, the source of all law, order, and authority, the uniter and ruler of mankind. Although his empire was essentially spiritual, it extended over all departments of life; for sovereignty over the soul of man implies sovereignty over the body, which is the condition of the soul's manifestation. This claim to spiritual and universal power is the central idea in the history of the papacy. It first asserted itself in the pontificate of Gregory the Great; it inspired Gregory VII. and Innocent III.; it animated the long struggle against the empire; it brought to the holy see princely donations of revenue and territory; it enabled the Riarios, the Borgias, the Medicis, and the Farnesi to conquer by violence and fraud a kingdom in the very heart of the peninsula; it kindled the fires of the inquisition; it proscribed the writings of Galileo and the poetry of Milton; it made permanent the intervention of foreign armies in Italy, stimulated the division of her territory and her people, and quenched their aspirations in the blood of patriots and martyrs. The same spirit now leads Pius IX. to resist the advancing waves of modern civilization, and causes him to oppose Victor Emmanuel in the reconstruction of Italy as a nation, as his predecessors opposed the Longobard kings, Frederick II., King Arduin, and other noble princes who strove to achieve the same object.

In the infancy of modern nations, the papal sovereignty, although involving spiritual servitude, was legitimate, because the papacy represented the mind of humanity, and was the only existing agency of progress. Then it stood forth the sole antagonist of the prevailing barbarism, the only beacon of moral and intellectual light. It preserved the treasures of Greek and Roman genius, fostered science, established the universities of Europe, summoned the arts to do homage to Christianity, and reared cathedrals and monuments in its honor; it sent forth armies of apostles throughout the world, and employed all human and divine powers for the moral education of man. Then the successors of St. Peter held in truth the keys of heaven and hell; they could arm the people and drain the treasuries of Europe for their holy wars, distribute continents and crowns among subject kings, cause emperors to kneel abjectly at their feet, and nations to tremble at their wrath.

But with the advance of civilization, when new principles and new forces were evolved, and new forms of society appeared, the papal power began to decline, as paganism had declined at the approach of Christianity. When the revival of letters awoke the human intellect from its long slumber, and the invention of printing opened the channels of thought; when the discovery of America widened the field of man's activity, and new languages became the germs of new nationalities, Rome ceased to be the centre of the moral world, and the voice of the great reformer found an echo in the hearts of the people. The reformation was the dawn of the great era of spiritual emancipation; to the papal authority it opposed the light which 'lighteth every man that cometh into the world;" to the rites of the church, the efficacy of moral agencies; to the perpetuity of the priesthood and the ecclesiastical votes, the everlasting responsibility of the human conscience; and to the hierachy the equality of men. Scholars, jurisconsults, and statesmen eagerly accepted the new principles; universities and legislative codes were enfranchised; the autonomy of the state was affirmed, the right of popular sovereignty asserted, and the revolutions of England, France, and America followed as successive acts of the great drama which opened with the burning of the bull of Leo before the gates of Wittenberg. The supremacy of human reason and of conscience was established; heresy, no longer a crime, became a sacred right, and the abandonment of an institution, now a barrier to human progress, a moral obligation. New methods and new sciences arose; a new literature and a new philosophy appeared; and Shakespeare, Goethe, Kant, and Hegel were hailed as kings and lords of the human mind. Now the press supersedes the oracle of St. Peter; priests, bishops, and councils give way to men of science, to scholars, artists, statesmen, and parliaments. Political economy succeeds theology; industrial and commercial activity displaces the old asceticism; new and more Christian codes are promulgated; the ballot-box supplants the papal bull; physical science develops new forces more spiritual than those of the legendary; the steam-engine and the electric telegraph prove far more beneficial to mankind than all the blessings dispensed "Urbi and Orbi" from the Vatican; and while an ambiguous word from the lips of Napoleon or the seizure of two rebel slaveholders by an American commodore spread alarm and consternation throughout Europe, all the maledictions of Pius IX., and the once dread thunders of Rome fall harmlessly upon an age which listens to them only with pity or scorn.

The papacy, resting on principles which are in direct antagonism to those of modern civilization, and having thus lost its hold on public opinion, has ceased to be a spiritual power, and is reduced to a mere external establishment. It is not ambition nor obstinacy which places Pius IX. in opposition to our age; but it is the duty of his position, the inevitable logic of the system which he represents, the nature of the power which he claims to have inherited from his predecessors. Should he admit the pre-eminence of individual reason over his authority, religious freedom, the freedom of the press, the sovereignty of the people, and other axioms of social science, he would at once renounce his pretensions to spiritual sovereignty, and cease to be pope. Claiming to enjoy the exclusive possession of immutable truth, to be the supreme guardian of justice, and to have the right, if not the power to enforce his faith upon mankind, "the supreme pontiff cannot," says Pius IX., in one of his last allocutions, "stretch out his right hand of friendship toward the civilization of the present, stoop to conditions with it, or bind himself to alliance therewith." This antagonism, which is inherent to the papal institution, is still more clearly defined by Gregory XVI., one of the most learned divines who has ever filled the papal chair, when in his encyclical letter of 1832, he declares, that "the universal church is distracted by whatever is new;" that "the regeneration of the church is simply absurd and injurious;" that "the opinion purporting that salvation may be secured through all Christian communions, provided man lives honestly and rightly, is a perverse doctrine propagated by the artifices of bad men;" that "the freedom of conscience is not only an absurd and erroneous maxim, but a delirium;" that "the freedom of the press is a baleful liberty, for which one cannot feel too much horror;" that "the separation of the state from the church, is injurious to both;" that "civil authority is given to governments, not only for temporal objects, but more particularly for the defence of the church;" and finally, that "the right of revolution is condemned by all human and divine laws."

Such is the attitude of the papal church in relation to the civilization of the 19th century. From its long domination, its assumption of divine prerogatives, and its denunciation of all reforms as attacks upon religion, the papacy in Italy has become identified with Christianity, which, as a religious faith, has now reached that point of decline which the paganism of Rome had attained in the age of Trajan—it has become an external and sensuous worship with the people, a subject of scepticism and indifference with the enlightened classes, and a matter of policy with the government. The assertion of Machiavelli, at the close of the 15th century, that "it was to the church that the Italians owed the loss of their religion as well as the divisions of their country,"* is even more true in our day. The identification of the genuine catholic elements of Christianity with what is purely exclusive and sectarian in the Roman church, has not only led to the degeneracy of the religious

* Machiavelli Discorsi sopra la Prima Deca di T. Livio. Lib. I., cap. 12.

sentiment of the people, but it strengthens now the pretensions of the pope, and weakens the position of the Italian government in their struggle for the possession of Rome.* As long as the papacy is identified with Christianity, all attempts to reconcile the church with the highest Christian civilization to which Italy aspires, must necessarily fail. The late proposal to guarantee to the pope the privileges of sovereignty, to his cardinals the dignity of princes, and to sustain his court from the finances of the State, is obviously in direct opposition to religious freedom, which recognizes no privileged sect and excludes all taxation for religious purposes; neither will such concessions satisfy the claims of the church or the religious and political interests of the country. The church can only be reconciled with the freedom of Italy, by cutting off the papal excrescence, and returning to its primitive organization; by recognizing its dependence on the state in all civil matters; by restoring the right of election to the clergy and the people; by finding its support in voluntary contributions; by transforming the hierarchy from a caste, which, in the words of Rosmini, "is now divided from society at large, with interests, language, laws, and customs of its own,"† into a free and independent ministry; by adopting, in short, the constitution of the principal churches in the United States, which finds its model in the apostolic times. Thus transformed, the freedom of the church would be secured by the free institutions of the state, the only guarantee which a genuine Christian church can demand, or a free government can give. But these reforms, which would destroy the existing papacy, it is in vain to expect; and it is therefore impossible for the state to abandon those rights over the church which are its only security against the encroachments of an institution which now, more than ever, is plotting against its liberties.

Whatever policy may be followed in regard to the papacy, whether the Roman question will be solved before or after the death of the present pope, Rome cannot long continue a papal

* See note C.

† Le Cinque Piaghe della Chiesa di Antonio Rosmini. Cap. I. See note D.

city, surrounded as she is by a free nation. Meanwhile, Italy, to achieve the freedom of the state, must proclaim the spiritual sovereignty of the individual conscience, the sole sovereignty under God, and thus secure the freedom of the citizens in religious matters. No truth is more clearly demonstrated by modern philosophy than that religious opinions belong essentially to the individual, and that, the state being incompetent to regulate the external acts dependent on those opinions, the existence of a national church or of a state religion is incompatible with free institutions. The power of the Roman emperors extended over the body and soul of the subject; but Christianity appeared to set free the divine element of the human mind, and to assert its natural sovereignty. Religion and science, two branches from the same root, were thus made free by the mission of the Redeemer, and the state has no more power over the one than over the other. There are moral elements in the nature of man which were particularly developed by the Gospel, and without which no society can flourish. But they have an absolute worth, independently of any sanction of government; they belong to a sphere infinitely superior to that of the state, and form an essential part of modern civilization. The human mind, if left alone, will bring supernatural influences to bear on society; but the state, as such, has no control over these influences, and the attempt to enforce it led to the persecution of the early Christians, brought heretics to the dungeons and the stake of the inquisition, subjected Catholics and dissenters to civil disabilities in Protestant countries, rendered Protestants odious to Catholic governments, and all believers in Christ outcasts among Mohammedans. "It is impossible," says Cavour, "to conceive a greater calamity for a civilized people, than to see civil and religious authority united in one hand, and that the hand of the government. The history of all ages and all countries establishes this fact; where these two authorities have been united, civilization has almost instantaneously ceased advancing, and has never failed to retrograde ultimately; the most odious of despotisms has been established;

and this result has happened equally whenever a sacerdotal caste has assumed temporal authority or whenever a caliph or sultan has assumed spiritual power. Everywhere this fatal confusion of authority has led to the same result." "The union of state and church renders society a hideous monster," says Macaulay, "cursed with one principle of sensation and two principles of volition, self-loathing and self-torturing—made up of parts which are driven by frantic impulse to inflict mutual pain, yet are doomed to feel whatever they inflict; which are divided by an irreconcilable hatred, yet are blended in an indissoluble identity;" and the distinguished writer illustrates this union by that wild Persian fable, in which "King Zohak gave the devil leave to kiss his shoulders. Instantly two serpents sprang out, which in the fury of hunger attacked his head, and attempted to get at his brain. Zohak pulled them away, and tore them with his nails; but he found that they were inseparable parts of himself, and that what he was lacerating was his own flesh.*

The separation of state and church, which was one of the chief objects of Cavour's policy, is a principle logically derived from the doctrines of the Reformation; but it is only in the United States that it bears its perfect fruit. Here religious liberty, incorporated with the character of the people, has become a basis of nationality far more firm than that which other nations seek in external conformity of worship; placing all denominations, Protestant and Catholic, on an equal footing, binding all to the laws of the state, it gives full scope to that competition which is the source of all progress, leaves them to provide for their own support and for the religious education of their communicants, and renders the clergy and the laity of all sects, though clad in different uniforms, soldiers of the same army, who, beneath the same flag of liberty, do battle against the common enemy, ignorance and wrong. Thus tolerance is promoted, Christian feeling nurtured, and civilization developed. It is only by adopting this genuine catholic system of

* "Church and State," by T. B. Macaulay.

religious freedom, that the reform proposed by Cavour may be accomplished, and a free church introduced into a free state. Then Italy will open a new era in the annals of liberty in Europe, and inaugurate a new Reformation, the consummation of that which more than three centuries ago wrested half Europe from the papal power; the more perfect, as the civilization of our age is more advanced than that of the 16th century.*

The discussion of the Roman question was succeeded in the parliament by the debate on the military force of the country, and particularly on the disbanding of the volunteers who had contributed so effectually to the deliverance of southern Italy. On this occasion Cavour was assailed with great bitterness by Garibaldi—an attack which was probably one of the most painful incidents of his life. We have already referred to the characteristic and political differences which separated these two leaders. The policy which put an end to the dictatorship of the great chieftain in Naples, had contributed still more to envenom his feeling toward Cavour. It must be admitted that all the details of that policy were by no means justifiable, and that the splendid achievements of Garibaldi, his lofty patriotism, his extreme sensibility, his virtues as well as his weaknesses, required on the part of the administration a delicate consideration, which has not always inspired the cabinet in its relations with the conqueror of Palermo and Naples. If, for the purpose of checking the disorders of the Neapolitan provinces, a new regime was required, it was not necessary to supplant him by men known to be obnoxious to him, much less to refuse to comply with his requests, his caprices even, as long as they did not impede the success of the great cause. The government of Turin, it is true, offered to him whatever he might desire for himself and his family. But with Garibaldi such an offer was more likely to give offence than satisfaction, particularly as his demands in behalf of his most devoted friends were disregarded, and even popular demonstrations in his favor prevented.

* See note E.

Granting, then, that the chieftain had some ground for complaint, had he allowed himself to be led by his generous nature he would have overlooked the errors of the administration, inasmuch as Cavour had ever shown that his opposition to him was inspired solely by the public necessities, not by any feeling of resentment or jealousy. Garibaldi was too true a patriot not to distinguish the cause of the nation from the men in power; and, ready to sacrifice himself to the former, he would have cheerfully submitted to all he might have considered as a slight or injustice. But, unhappily, on leaving Naples he had fallen again under the control of ill advisers, whose influence was exerted to increase rather than to allay his animosity. This was the more easy, as the administration of Naples which had succeeded his dictatorship was far from remedying the evils which had led to the change. A people whose character partakes of the volcanic nature of their soil; whose mental structure, although substantially Italian, is tinged with Greek peculiarities, blended with a strong tendency to superstition, the legacy of the Spanish domination; and whose spirit has been crushed for centuries under the degrading influences of bigotry and despotism, the Neapolitans could not at once identify themselves with the more positive characteristics of the northern Italians. Had it been possible to surround Garibaldi with more enlightened and patriotic counsellors, it would doubtless have been more wise, in that period of transition, to have retained him as governor over a people who still regard with awe the miracle of the transformation of the blood of St. Januarius. A hero of almost supernatural prestige was best fitted to counteract the influence of the priesthood over the lower classes. But Cavour could not intrust the administration to that party whose direction had proved so dangerous to the national cause; and in seeking to avert this evil he incurred others not less mischievous. The revolutionary elements acquired new strength from the discontent which arose from the superseding of their representative, and Cavour now found himself opposed in Naples not only by the republicans, but by the clergy and the other allies of the dethroned Bourbon, who had found refuge within the walls of the Quirinal, where he occupied himself in enlisting into his service brigands from all quarters of Europe, whom he let loose upon the Neapolitan territory, eager for pillage and blood, fit champions of his rights. Amidst these difficulties it is not surprising that order was not at once established, especially when it is considered that Cavour resolutely declined to proclaim martial law, however justified by the necessities of the time, since he believed that in the end national progress would be more benefited by the excesses of liberty than by the coercion of despotism, and the event seemed to prove the wisdom of his policy.

In all revolutionary periods, utopian theorists, empirical politicians, disappointed office-seekers, men of definite and men of vague ideas, guided by antipathy or by sympathy, by ambition or patriotism, although divided among themselves, will on occasions rally around a common centre to present a strong front of opposition to the government. So in the first Italian parliament these various elements united, and looked upon Garibaldi as their leader. Before the elections they proposed to nominate him a candidate in many districts, in order to display a powerful manifestation against the policy of Cavour, particularly against the French alliance, to which they attributed the delay in the settlement of the Roman question. Garibaldi, aware that his place was not in the parliament, at first declined all nominations, and it was only through the entreaties of his friends that he finally consented to represent one of the districts of Naples. The decrees of the government in relation to the disbanding of the volunteers had produced great disaffection, and he now urged their repeal, the maintenance of the volunteers on a war footing, and the general arming of the country—measures which the government could not adopt, in view of the complications they would involve with foreign powers.

Public sentiment was divided on this subject, and the agitations which followed, threatening to disturb the concord to which the past successes were chiefly due, Baron Ricasoli proposed to introduce the question before the parliament, in the hope of bringing about a reconciliation between the two leaders. On the 18th of April, 1861, the day appointed for that discussion, Garibaldi for the first time made his appearance in the chamber of deputies. He entered the hall clad in his worn red shirt, surrounded by his friends, amidst the cheers of the house and the galleries. Baron Ricasoli soon opened the debate, by depicting in glowing colors the triumphs which thus far had crowned the efforts of the Italian people, and, deploring the fatal misunderstanding which had arisen between the two men who had rendered the greatest service to the country, with patriotic earnestness he called upon the house to inquire into its cause, and demanded from the ministry that information should be laid before the chamber on the condition of the regular army and the volunteers. The secretary of war accordingly brought forward a report on the national forces, and strove to demonstrate that the late decrees were favorable to the volunteers, and best calculated to secure their future services.

Garibaldi then rose, and thanking Ricasoli for having introduced a subject of such vital importance to him, as it regarded the interests of his companions in arms, he admitted the disagreement existing between him and Cavour, but he declared that he was always ready to yield whenever the welfare of the country demanded it. Had he closed his speech at this point he would have won the day; but, new to parliamentary usages, and instigated by some of his most reckless adherents, he allowed himself to be carried away by his ill feeling. He repeated his former taunt that Cavour had made him a foreigner in his native land; he reproached him for having blighted his success in Naples by his cold and baneful influence; and rising to the climax of bitterness, he accused him of having instigated civil war, and of being the enemy of his country. Wounded to the quick, Cavour rose to protest. But the house protested for him; the members sprang to their feet as one man, and amidst the general confusion and shouts of an indignant assembly, the chairman declared the house adjourned. This protest found an echo through the whole civilized world; and the press of Europe as well as of America—indeed all who felt an interest in the cause of Italian liberty—while they bestowed on the great chieftain the tribute of their unbounded admiration, were unanimous in the expression of their sorrow that he who represented the arm of Italy should have indulged in such an attack upon him who represented the national mind.

The house being called to order, General Bixio, an ardent patriot, a warm friend of Garibaldi, and one of his bravest lieutenants, made an earnest appeal to him not to sacrifice to his feeling the holy cause in which they were all with equal patriotism engaged; he implored Cavour to forgive his chief, and both to unite their efforts in accomplishing the great work which Providence had intrusted to their hands. Cavour was first to accept the proposed reconciliation; and with his usual coolness and urbanity, he offered not only forgiveness but oblivion for what had just occurred; he had even the magnanimity to justify the attack of his adversary, remarking that "from the grief he himself had felt, when he thought it his duty to advise the king to cede Nice and Savoy, he could well understand the feelings of the general, and the resentment he had shown." Would to God, that the reconciliation which at first was accepted by Garibaldi had been permanent! But while the house, by passing the resolution of Ricasoli by an overwhelming majority, expressed its adhesion to the policy of Cavour, the great chieftain still continued to distrust the statesman. Nor was the attempt made by Victor Emmanuel to change his feeling more successful. They met indeed at Moncalieri, where they had been invited by the king; but while Cavour, too high-souled for rancor, cheerfully offered his hand in friendship, and never ceased to express his appreciation of the high qualities of Garibaldi, the latter, always reflecting the opinion of those who surrounded him, failed to reciprocate the feeling except for the moment.

Although Cavour came out of this conflict victorious, he felt to the heart the wound which had been inflicted upon him, rendered still more severe by the effort to conceal it. From that time a change took place in his countenance. He had already manifested symptoms of declining health, and suffered from repeated attacks of congestion of the brain. The great amount of labor which he performed, the immense responsibilities of his position, his bitter disappointment at the abrupt termination of the war, his intense anxiety arising from the unsettled affairs of Naples, Venice, and Rome, the attacks of those from whom he expected a cordial support, all combined to tax to the utmost his exquisite sensibility; while his unhealthy manner of life, his long fasts alternating with hasty meals, his close confinement, and the neglect of physical exercise, all contributed to undermine his iron constitution. His eyes now lost their brilliancy, his once florid complexion assumed an unnatural hue, and his habitual cheerfulness was succeeded by fits of melancholy and nervous excitability. For the first time he complained of fatigue, of his inability to rest; and he confessed to a friend that "he felt his frame giving way beneath his mind and will, which still urged it on," and expressed a wish that time might be allowed him to finish his work. "Then," said he, "I should care little for what happened; indeed, I should be glad to die." Still he worked on with redoubled zeal to the last. He was every day at his post in the parliament, answering questions, initiating the new house into the proceedings of constitutional government, urging forward measures best adapted to accomplish the unity of the nation, and explaining his policy with increased power and earnestness, as if a secret voice told him it was the legacy he was to bequeath to his country. As the head of the executive department, his labors were still greater; the sudden annexation of so many new provinces increased his duties to a prodigious extent. Old abuses were to be done away with, new institutions introduced, clashing interests reconciled, finances systematized, taxes revised, ways and means provided, the codes reformed, railroads marked out and built, telegraphs extended, the army and navy increased, every department reorganized, and, in short, order created out of chaos.

As minister of foreign affairs, the whole burden of the complicated relations with other countries rested upon him; and he was forced to keep a constant watch over the chess-board of European diplomacy, in order that he might influence the movements of friendly powers, ward off the attacks of enemies, and seize the moment in which he might checkmate the emperor of Austria and the government of Rome. In fact, he had the control of a titanic revolution, which his position obliged him to direct solely through diplomatic skill and energy.

This burden of the whole nation in its transition state would have broken down a frame of even greater endurance. Previous to the adjournment of the great national festival, to be celebrated for the first time in the beginning of June, 1861, the vast amount of business to be transacted rendered the sittings of the parliament unusually laborious, and strained to their utmost tension the already overwrought faculties of Cavour. On the 29th of May, the last day of his public life, he passed the morning at the department of state; in the afternoon he addressed the chamber on various topics, and the discussion turning on the claims of the volunteers, he heartily supported the motion for conciliation, declaring that all who had fought for Italy, whatever might have been their political antecedents and opinions, deserved well of the country. On the same evening he was seized with a chill, which continued through the night, and in the morning, according to his custom in similar cases, he himself prescribed bleeding. On the morning of the 31st of May his condition was so far improved that he insisted on giving audiences, and summoned to his bedside the minister of the viceroy of Naples, who had just arrived from that city. An exciting conversation of two hours brought on a relapse, with new and more dangerous symptoms; and on Sunday, the 2d of June, after a medical consultation, he was once more bled, and the operation was repeated again and again. For this method of treatment much blame has been attached to his physicians, particularly in the United States and in England. But it was pursued in accordance with the wishes of Cavour himself, who, having experienced relief from it in other similar attacks, and having very little faith in medical skill, insisted that this remedy alone should be applied. The true cause of the disease which closed his career, whatever form it may have assumed, was overwork; and it is doubtful if his exhausted nature possessed sufficient power of reaction under any mode of treatment.

On Thursday, the 4th of June, alarming symptoms began to appear in the sufferer, and the news of his dangerous condition spreading through Turin, cast a deep gloom over the city. The streets leading to his palace were soon filled with a silent and sorrowful multitude, eagerly awaiting reports from the sick chamber. Those who but the day before had been his bitter opponents, now laying aside all party considerations, mingled with that anxious crowd; eyes which had regarded him with coldness or envy, were now wet with tears, and many a one among that throng would willingly have given himself a sacrifice to save the life on which the fate of the nation seemed to hang. And when, toward the last, that deep silence was broken by the sound of the bell of the viaticum, alternating with the prayers for the dying, and the solemn procession of torch-bearers, led by the good Frà Giacomo bearing the host, was seen entering the palace, a sob of anguish arose from that multitude, as if the last hope of the country was about to be extinguished forever. Within, beneath the roof under which he was born, conscious that his last hour has come, yet calm, confident, and serene, lies the dying statesman; dying at the close of the first festival of the national birthday, thus rendered doubly sacred to posterity; surrounded by his household and friends, in the embrace of the king to whom he had given the crown of Italy; amidst the anxiety of all Europe, expressed by the hourly telegrams received from the various capitals; dying as he lived—an honest man, a true patriot, opposing to the last the papal church, whose sacraments, the symbols of Christianity, he receives in spite of her excommunication, thus showing that he can be a Christian without being a papist. Whether in the full possession of his faculties or in the wanderings of delirium, no bitterness or rancor escapes his lips, but he speaks words of cheer and consolation to his friends, assuring them that all is saved, that Italy is secure; and as the morning of the 6th of June dawns, he gradually sinks, still absorbed in the one thought of his country for whose greatness he had lived; and, uttering faintly and at intervals the darling names of Italy, Rome, and Venice, his glorious spirit passes away.

The tidings of Cavour's death rang throughout the peninsula like the knell of the nation, and for a moment the whole Italian people seemed to have been struck by the same blow which had prostrated their great leader in his prime and vigor. At Turin the consternation was overwhelming; the whole city was shrouded in mourning. The hum of commerce and business was no longer heard; the occupations of ordinary life were for the time suspended; and the pervading silence was broken only by the thousand bells which rang forth their mournful funeral peals. In the great hall of Cavour palace the remains lay in state, and the constituted bodies and the whole people thronged thither to pay their last tribute to the illustrious dead, and to gaze once more on his beloved features. On the 8th of June, the funeral took place with all the pomp of military display, and with more than royal honors. Placed on a magnificent car, and attended by the troops under arms, with all the splendid pageantry of the church and state, followed by senators, deputies, ministers, dignitaries of the state, the courts, the municipal, scientific, commercial, and religious corporations, amidst the solemn chants of the clergy, the roll of the muffled drums, the thunder of artillery, and the mourning of a whole people, the form of Cavour was borne, through the avenues of the city, draped with black and strown with funeral flowers, to the church of the Madonna degli Angeli. The king requested the privilege of enshrining the sacred remains of his minister in the royal vaults of Superga; Turin claimed the honor of guarding the relics of her greatest son; and Florence opened her pantheon of Santa Croce, and asked to place them by the side of those of Machiavelli and Galileo. But Cavour had long before expressed a wish to be laid in the tomb of his ancestors; and in the little village of Santena, within the family chapel, his honored dust reposes.

The deep emotion which the death of Cavour everywhere occasioned is fresh in our memory. It was not alone the result of that sympathy with which all civilized nations regarded Italy, but it arose from an appreciation of the high personal qualities of the great patriot. Every freeman, whether in Europe or in America, felt that in him he had lost a friend. The parliament of England resounded with the praises of the illustrious dead; the emperor of France, true to his friendship, hastened to recognize over his grave the kingdom of Italy; and the people of the United States, forgetting for a moment the calamities of civil war, through the countless voices of their press gave utterance to the universal sentiment of regret—a sentiment profoundly echoed in the hearts of those Italians who had left their native land in despair, when no ray of hope pierced the gloom of the future, who from these distant shores watched with intense emotion the resurrection of their country as he raised her into life, and who in their absence found their only consolation in seeing their beloved Italy again take her place among the nations. Let the Italian people follow the teaching and example of their great statesman, and when generations shall have passed away, and the fruits of the unity and independence which he secured shall have reached their maturity, the lonely tomb of Santena will become the Mount Vernon of Italy, the sacred shrine to which pilgrims will come to do homage to the memory of him who gave life and freedom to a nation.

In person Cavour was below the medium height; his figure was strongly built; his brow massive and intellectual; his eyes were clear and penetrating; and over his firmly set mouth a smile half ironical and half humorous habitually played. His whole face indicated the strength, the sensibility, and vivacity of his character, and faithfully reflected all his emotions; in which respect alone he was no diplomatist. Indeed, his unconscious outward manifestations of pleasure or dissatisfaction were so marked, that the state of his mind could be easily interpreted by those who watched him even as he passed along the streets.

His private life was quiet and laborious. To the last, he continued to rise between four and five o'clock in the morning. He devoted the first hour to his personal affairs, and the remainder of the day to his duties at the department, or in the parliament. After a late dinner he returned to his occupations, and remained engaged until past midnight. He found his chief recreation in his occasional visits to his estates at Leri, where, laying aside the cares of state, he delighted to mingle with his tenants, to discuss with them the best methods of agriculture, to direct their labors, and to provide for their comfort and improvement. He was never married. When in the city, he lived with his elder and only brother, the Marquis Gustavo di Cavour, a member of the parliament, a man of great nobleness of character, and of high intellectual attainments, but from whose religious views he differed widely. Cavour considered Christianity, in its relation to social existence, as a religion of love and progress; and while he strove to infuse into the nation those catholic principles of life, he left to his brother the study of its metaphysical and theological aspects. He was deeply attached to his family; to his surviving nephew he bequeathed the bulk of his fortune, and he desired to be laid by the side of the other, who had fallen in the war of independence. In manners, he was simple and charming; his conversation was brilliant and witty. He was genial and fond of frolic and fun, although his temper was passionate, and he was at times imperious and intolerant of opposition even from his best friends. But this was evanescent; and, either wrong or right, with his equals or subordinates, with friends or foes, he was always the first to seek a reconciliation whenever he had given offence. His personal prejudices and antipathies were not deeply rooted, and easily gave way, while the great power of satire which he possessed he freely used as a weapon, not as a vehicle of ill-nature. He was accessible to the humblest citizen. He was kind, generous, and tender-hearted, and delighted in acts of benevolence, many of which he performed in secret. Firm in the consciousness of right, he was superior to flattery or censure; and although, as the moral dictator of the nation, he generally chose for his subordinates men of mediocrity, laborious and submissive, rather than those who were remarkable for genius or personal independence, he appreciated talent and patriotism even in his adversaries, whom he often intrusted with important offices.

As a debater, Cavour was not distinguished by brilliancy of language, imagery of style, modulation of voice or elegance of gesture, but by affluence of thought and general knowledge, by wit, and force of reasoning and expression. His speeches were more synthetic than analytic, dealing with a subject in all its principles and relations rather than in its details, and more resembling philosophical essays on practical affairs than the special pleadings of the lawyer or the effusions of a rhetorician. Clear, precise, and logical, he lacked the grandeur of Webster, the inspiration of Clay, and the finish of Everett; but he fixed the attention by his well defined premises, breadth of treatment, power of argument, aptness of illustration, naturalness of style, and almost mathematical sequence of ideas. He possessed in a remarkable degree the faculty of anticipating the thoughts of others long before they were expressed; and when a dull speaker or an imprudent friend had the floor, his general uneasiness and restless motion manifested his impatience. Over the house he exerted an almost absolute sway, and his speeches, especially those on free trade, the alliance with England and France, the Roman question, and on other subjects of equal importance, will remain enduring monuments of his parliamentary ability.

The grandeur of Cavour's character as a statesman must be estimated by the magnitude of his object, the boldness and the prudence with which he executed his designs, and the extraordinary power which he possessed of foreseeing results and of converting obstacles into means. He combined the originality and depth of a theorist with the practical genius of a true reformer; he understood the character of the age in which he lived, and made it tributary to his great purposes. He made self-government the object of legislation, political economy the source of liberty, and liberty the basis of nationality. Aware that neither revolution nor conservatism alone could produce the regeneration of his country, he opposed them in their separate action, while he grasped them both with a firm hand, yoked them together, and led them on to conquest. He saw that Italian independence could only be attained through the aid of foreign alliance; he recognized in Napoleon III. the personification of organized revolution, and the natural ally of the Italian people; and the work, which he foreshadowed in the union of the Sardinian troops with the armies of England and France in the Crimea, and for which he laid the foundation in the congress of Paris, was achieved with the victories of Magenta and Solferino, and the recognition of the new kingdom of Italy.

More than five centuries ago, when Dante beheld the splendor of Italian civilization obscured by civil war and foreign oppression, his beautiful country divided into petty sovereignties, distracted by mutual jealousies, the fair provinces of the south convulsed by the intrigues of the heirs of Charles of Anjou, "Rome mixing two governments that ill assort," Florence disturbed by demagogues, Venice misruled by aristocrats, Milan harassed by Guelph lords, Verona by Ghibelline masters, Pisa armed against Genoa, Genoa against Venice, the papacy struggling against the empire, the empire against the papacy, and the fury of discord everywhere raging, he poured forth, in sublime strains which have echoed through the ages, his warning to nations against the calamities of disunion. In vain he strove to unite those discordant elements into harmony and nationality; and to this cause devoted his genius, his love, his religion, his life, and consecrated his labors as poet and soldier, as magistrate and statesman. In vain he called upon Albert and Henry VII., and appealed to Can della Scala lord of Verona, and to other Italian princes for aid. Broken down by the disasters of his country, disappointed in his love, his property confiscated, exiled from his native city, a fugitive under sentence of death, wandering through the peninsula, and proving everywhere—

> "How salt the savor is of others' bread,
> How hard the passage, to descend and climb
> By others' stairs"—

he reached Ravenna to breathe his last in the bitterness of sorrow and despair. But rejoice, O illustrious shade! The sacred fire of patriotism which burns in thy immortal song, has at last kindled the hearts of thy countrymen. Thy lofty aspirations, borne on the wings of thy divine poetry, like invisible hosts, have led thy country on to liberty and union; thy noble dream is at last fulfilled. Behold the papal throne crumbling to its foundations, the imperial sceptre broken asunder, and the Italian cities, upon whom thou didst lay thy unmerciful scourge, with the torches of discord extinguished, like a band of sisters, arrayed under the standard of that Emmanuel, whom in thy vision thou didst foresee.* Bend down, O immortal genius of Italy! bend down from thy paradise, where "in the light supreme thou livest;" receive into thy bosom the spirit of the great Italian whom we mourn; who has wrought thy divine poem into thy nation's history; who has accomplished the work to which thou didst give thy life. Receive him, and, as once Beatrice led thee, be thou his guide through those realms where founders of nations, champions of liberty, martyrs and benefactors of humanity, forever dwell in glorious immortality.

* See Note F.

NOTES.

NOTE A.

The following extract from a letter addressed by Cavour to the writer of this discourse, dated July 9th, 1859, two days before the interview of Villafranca, proves how bright were his anticipations at that time, and how highly he appreciated the sympathy expressed by the American people for the Italian cause: "The unanimous expressions of sympathy and affection which all civilized nations bestowed upon the defenders of Italian independence, show that our cause is closely connected with the vast interests of justice and civilization. The country which gave birth to Washington has always been the first to give us substantial proofs of its benevolence. Following its example, and aided, as America was, by the generous armies of France, we shall reach our goal, and Italy, having secured her independence, will bring again to the assembly of nations the tribute of her activity in industry, science, and arts."

NOTE B.

Prominent among the writers of this class is Lamartine, who, in his "Cours familier de Littérature, 61 Entretien, 1861," seems to have proposed to himself the object of exciting the jealousy of the French people against the Italian movement. Commonplace arguments, borrowed from the upholders of the Austrian and papal governments, form the substance of his pages, in which party spirit is ill concealed under the charm of style. He maintains that a confederation is the normal state of the peninsula, and describes Italian unity as a Sardinian conquest, the result of the ambition of the house of Savoy, aided by the intrigues of England, who thus plots against the security of France. Omitting to state the facts on which his assumptions rest, it is difficult to enter into any criticism of his "Diplomatic Littérature," the main object of which is so evidently to attack the policy of the French emperor. The plan of Lamartine, consisting in dividing the country into various small sovereignties, would doubtless make it subservient to the interests of other nations; but united Italy, a maritime power with a population of twenty-six millions, would be much more likely to be regarded by England as a rival than as a tool. When Lamartine, the republican of 1848, talks of the equilibrium of nations, international right, *Italian nationalities*, the necessity of an alliance between France and Austria, and the respect due to diplomatic treaties, in language which would become a Metternich, we recall the opinion expressed by Cavour on that writer as early as 1845, when the events of the following years had not yet reduced to its just proportions his statesmanship. "This great poet," wrote Cavour, "and illustrious writer, has hitherto shown too little power of appreciating the positive and practical side of life for his opinion to carry much weight. The very wealth and power of imagination to which his great literary success is due, seem to be insurmountable obstacles to his disciplining his mind, and submitting it to the severe exigencies of science and logic. He is disqualified, therefore, for forming any precise or valid opinion with regard to questions which relate to the policy of the day."

NOTE C.

In discussing the Roman question, it is important to insist on this distinction between those genuine principles of Christianity, which constitute the basis of the Roman church and those of the papacy, an accidental and temporary form, through which the Christian religion manifested itself in ages bygone. The confounding of the divine and human elements of religion, of the absolute Christian idea with its historical manifestations, has ever been the source of religious despotism, and continues to be the great impediment to the full realization of Italian unity and independence. The spiritual sovereignty of the papacy is assumed as an essential element of Christianity, both by those writers who maintain that the temporal power is a necessary condition for the free exercise of the spiritual jurisdiction, and by those who consider that power obnoxious to the true interests of the papal institution. All these writers, although apparently belonging to opposite schools, admit *a priori* the spiritual power of the papacy, as a principle inherent to Christianity, thus ignoring alike the apodictical conclusions of modern philosophy, which have long since swept away that assumption from social science, and the fact that that principle is rejected by the more enlightened half of Christendom, which to this open disregard owes its moral and economical supremacy.

Among the writers of the papal school we may mention Guizot, whose recent book, "L'Église et la Société Chrétienne en 1861," is based on this confusion. It is not surprising that the professional defenders of the papal see should endeavor to perpetuate this fundamental error; they can follow no other course, since the papal system excludes all possibility of questioning the principle on which it rests. But that a Protestant and a philosophical writer should base his work on such premises, is not to be accounted for, even on the ground of opposition to the policy of the emperor of France, which has obviously led Guizot to the support of the papal throne. Passing over the manifest hostility toward Italy, which causes him, in common with Lamartine and other French writers, to attribute the recent events in the peninsula to the ambition of the house of Savoy, and otherwise to misrepresent the Italian movement, we cannot refrain from pointing out his mode of reasoning on the papal question. From the assumption that traditional Christianity is everywhere attacked by rationalists and critics, Guizot concludes that it is the duty of all Christian churches to defend its different forms, and therefore to stand by their sister of Rome, whose external organization, including the temporal power of the pope, is a condition of its existence. Had the author of "The History of Civilization in Europe" analyzed the Christian elements which the Roman church possesses in common with other churches, and which lie at the foundation of the present civilization; had he pointed out the zeal through which that church strives to propagate its faith, the pre-eminence given to æsthetic and symbolic agencies in the divine worship, the charitable institutions, which, nurtured by the church, are the ornament of southern Europe, and the elasticity of mind through which many of its members escape, although at the expense of their logic, the evil consequences of the system; had he urged the preservation of the genuine elements of the Roman church, he would have secured the sympathy of all truly liberal minds, who regard the Christian religion as the universal bond uniting all Christians, and which is destined to embrace all mankind. Such an analysis, however, would have led him to a conclusion quite different from that to which he arrives. He would have seen that the papacy, both in its spiritual and temporal attributes, has long since ceased to be a part of that catholicism which is the characteristic of all truth, and that it is only by an inveterate abuse of terms that it can be confounded with the catholic religion. An institution which, from its very essence, excludes from the pale of Christianity all dissenting communions, claims jurisdiction over all Christians, whether they acknowledge or repudiate its authority, and which, disregarding all distinction between fundamental and secondary tenets, holds as equally heretical those who reject the universal dogmas of the creation, incarnation, and redemption, and those who deny their assent to its own doctrines on the infallibility of the church, transubstantiation, confession, purgatory, and the like—such an institution cannot be properly called catholic or universal. Much less can it be expected that other churches should come to the support of those exclusive principles, which they consider as opposed to the gospel as well as to their own existence. Equally sophistical appears the plea of Guizot in behalf of the temporal power as necessary to the freedom of the church. If other churches can exist and flourish although deprived of all temporalities, it cannot be seen how a kingdom is necessary to the Roman church. Religious authority derives its legitimacy only from the free will of those who grant it, and excludes therefore all external power for its enforcement. The freedom of the papacy, involving the servitude of Italy, is not freedom but despotism; and the arguments employed by Guizot in the defence of such a cause fall to the ground, like those of the slaveholders of the South, who attempt to justify their rebellion against the freest government in the world, under the plea that their liberty is infringed upon, understanding for this liberty the power of extending human slavery over the American continent. In advocating the cause of papal liberty, Guizot advocates the cause of slavery in Italy, not that of Christianity.

While the defenders of the papacy, by confounding it with Christianity, are brought into open conflict with the Italian nationality, those writers who on the same ground strive to reconcile the papacy with Italy, compromise the claims of both. Passaglia in his "Pro Caussa Italica ad Episcopos Catholicos," professing his entire subjection to the spiritual sovereignty of the pope, which he considers essential to Christianity, contends that the papal temporalities are an impediment to the exercise of spiritual jurisdiction, and insists that the former should be renounced for the preservation of the latter. This view is common to other writers of the Catholic party in Italy, among whom are many priests, who, like Passaglia, having sustained with heroic devotion the papal system until the national cause seemed likely to triumph, now give to it this qualified support. The distinction between the spiritual and temporal power is the pivot upon which the arguments of those writers turn. Let the pope, say they, confine himself to his religious avocations, and from the Vatican rule his spiritual kingdom. Let the Italian government take possession of Rome, and from the Quirinal preside over the temporal interests of the nation, and the reconciliation of the papacy and Italy will be an accomplished fact. A beautiful arrangement, if it did not rest entirely on a mental abstraction, upon which it is impossible to build up a social reform. The distinction between the spiritual and temporal power, as understood by Passaglia and his companions, is but a relic of the scholastic philosophy, founded on the idea of an opposition existing between the soul and body, the former being subject to the authority of the pope, the latter to that of the emperor; and as the soul was regarded as the mistress of the body, so the papacy logically claimed right of domination over rulers and people. This claim gave rise to the long struggle between the papacy and the empire. Happily since that time philosophy has made some progress. Since then psychology and physiology have established the fact of the unity and the indivisibility of human nature; they have shown that the body is but the necessary condition of the soul's manifestation, and that not only no opposition, but perfect harmony exists between the two. Meanwhile ontology and ideology revived the ancient doctrine of Plato, corroborated by the teaching of the Gospel, of the immanent presence of the Absolute to the human mind; a presence through which some of the prerogatives of the Deity are communicated to the intellectual creature, which thus is made self-sovereign, and independent in all spiritual matters.

To grant spiritual sovereignty to the pope or to any human organization, is to recognize the right of spiritual despotism. If such sovereignty is not a fiction but a reality, it necessarily extends over the spiritual faculties of man; it involves the control of what is free and uncontrollable; it implies the subjection of the whole man; it excludes all other sovereignties; and tending to unite the race under its sway, it must trample of necessity upon the right of nationality. Thus the papacy is antagonistic to intellectual and religious liberty, the sovereignty of the people, and the right of nationality, which are the characteristic features of modern civilization. We go farther, and say that Passaglia and the other theologians of the new school cannot, consistently with their system, discuss the claims of the papacy, since spiritual power includes in itself the absolute right of defining its own nature, its limits and conditions. Add to this, that the church, according to papal doctrine, is a divinely appointed institution, endowed with a constitution of its own, with a determined order, which renders its system one and complete. The preservation of this hierarchical order is necessary to the preservation of the church itself; and those who presume to substitute for that authority their own private judgment, destroy the economy of the ecclesiastical establishment of Rome. When Passaglia therefore accumulates authorities from the Bible and the fathers, to contradict the claims of the papacy, however right he may be, he cannot call himself a follower of the system of which the papal church is the representative. As long as he professes himself subject to the papal authority, he will be properly reminded that it does not belong to a subordinate to dispute the rights of him who has the power of loosing and binding, who is the teacher and the shepherd, while he (Passaglia) is but a disciple and a sheep, bound to follow, not allowed to lead. The fact that even those who are more earnest in supporting the papal system destroy it in their attempt to limit it, shows that spiritual sovereignty has lost all reality, and has become only a name. Many of the politicians in Italy, knowing of religious matters only what they have learned from their nurses, or from the hearsay of papal theology, in the struggle in which they are engaged, profess great reverence and veneration for the papal see as a spiritual power, evidently fearing that the disregard for that power should be considered as a disregard for Christianity. Happily human nature is more logical and sincere than politicians and theologians, and we trust more in its development than in the artifices of the former, or in the quibbles of the latter, not only for a speedy solution of the Roman question, but particularly for that intellectual emancipation which is the first condition of the regeneration of Italy. Let the enlightened classes abandon the highly immoral practice of extolling an institution whose dogmas they do not believe, and many of whose precepts they daily violate; let them shake off that mental lethargy, which a long reign of despotism has fastened upon them; let them purify their religious sentiment through the light of genuine Christianity, which is essentially rational, moral, and civilizing; let them be sincere, consistent, and have the moral courage to act according to their belief. Then, and then only, will they be able to lead the people in the path of modern civilization, which was open to mankind through the triumph of human reason over papal tradition.

NOTE D.

The work of Rosmini, "Le cinque piaghe della Chiesa," in which the wounds of the church are typified by those of Christ on the cross, is an important production, not only for its subject, but also for the name of its writer and the circumstances under which it was published. No man has done so much for the interests of the papacy as Rosmini. A priest, a theologian, a philosopher, and the founder of a religious order, he may be considered as one of the greatest luminaries which have ever adorned the church. Although his philosophical principles, if logically followed, would have led him to renounce his allegiance to the papal sovereignty, his theological system checked the flight of his genius, and caused him to sacrifice his rational theories to his religious tenets, for the support of an authority which is the antithesis of all rationality. In Rosmini we must distinguish two individualities, the priest and the philosopher; the one humble, submissive, obedient, and self-sacrificing; the other self-reliant, bold, and independent. While the one recognized the supremacy of the individual mind, made rational by the innate and immanent presence of an absolute, objective, immutable, and universal truth, the infallible criterion of knowledge, and the supreme rule of action, the other bowed submissively to the claims of the papal institution, which he believed of an equally divine origin. With him this submission was the effect of his genuine piety, not the result of habit, interest, ignorance, scepticism, or mental lethargy, which so often combine to deprive men of all moral courage, and to hold them in false positions. He was, however, too philosophical to close his eyes to the abuses of the church, and too religious not to desire their removal. In 1832 he prepared the work alluded to, which, although strictly orthodox, and written in a meek and loving spirit, he was unable to publish until the accession of Pius IX., whom he regarded as destined "to renovate both the age and the church." He took a prominent part in the liberal movement at first headed by the present pope, and he was sent by Charles Albert ambassador to Rome to establish the basis of a confederacy among the Italian princes. He had nearly accomplished his mission, and had been named to the cardinalate, when Pius IX., obliged by the necessity of his position to retrace the steps which he had taken in the path of reform, fled to Gaeta, whither Rosmini followed him. But he soon found the futility of all efforts to infuse new life into an institution which claims absolute power from God, and to be irresponsible to men. He fell into disgrace, was arrested, and sent to Naples under military escort; he was then exiled from southern Italy, while his book on the wounds of the church was condemned.

The five wounds of the church, according to Rosmini, are, 1st, the separation of the priesthood from the people; 2d, the ignorance of the priests; 3d, the transformation of the bishops into feudal lords, divided among themselves, striving for wealth and power, and holding a despotic sway over *the low clergy;* 4th, the nomination of bishops abandoned to lay power, a necessary effect of the church having become a "terrestrial dominion;" 5th, the control of ecclesiastical property by the state, the inevitable result of its feudal tenure. To remedy these evils, Rosmini proposes, 1st, that the wall of separation existing between the priesthood and the people should be removed, and that the use of a dead language in divine service, which renders the people utterly deaf to the words addressed to them by the mother church, should be abandoned; 2d, that the standard of priestly education should be raised in accordance with the requirements of the age; 3d, that the bishops should return to their primitive organization, disentangle themselves from political parties and feudal pretensions, and strive to make the episcopate an object of attraction for pious and enlightened men, and not for worldly intriguers as it is at present; 4th, that the elections of bishops and the administration of the church should be restored to the clergy and the people, to whom they originally belonged, and that the bishops and priests, ceasing to confine themselves to the formalities and shows of worship should become again the confidants, the friends, and the fathers of the faithful; 5th, that the clergy should return to the spontaneous contributions of the people, as the only proper means of sustaining ecclesiastical establishments.

Had Rosmini traced the evils of the church to their legitimate origin, he would have found that they arose from the very nature of the papacy, and that the reforms he proposed could only be accepted by accepting the principle of the Reformation, which, destroying the papal sovereignty, has restored to the clergy and the laity their personal responsibility, and rendered ecclesiastical institutions capable of progress. The condemnation of the book of Rosmini affords another evidence of the utter impossibility of introducing reform into the papal system. He himself seems to have admitted this impossibility, when, complying with the first duty of a believer in the church, he submitted to the papal sentence, and disavowed all that was condemned in his work. Assuming that the papacy was the foundation of the Catholic church, and that this alone was the church of Christ, he could not do otherwise than submit. Those who condemn his submission are either unacquainted with the requirements of the papal church, or disregard the duty of consistency. Between Rosmini, who humbly bows to the papal authority, and Lamennais, who openly rebels against it, there is no course which a logical mind can accept. However we may deplore the humiliation to which Rosmini was subjected by his religious faith, his transcendent merit cannot be denied. We close these remarks with the following passage, through which we first presented his name to American scholars:

"It may be allowed to the writer of this paper to introduce to the acquaintance of American readers the venerated name of this great philosopher, a name which recalls to his mind the sweetest recollections of his life, and excites in his heart the deepest grief for his untimely death, which deprived Italy of one of her noblest sons, and science of one of its most gifted devotees. Devoted as a priest, refined as a scholar, sound as a statesman, sublime as a thinker, humble as a Christian, and bold as a philosopher, Rosmini united in himself in a high degree many qualities, any of which would be sufficient to convey to posterity the name of its possessor. The acuteness and breadth of his mind were only equalled by the extent of his learning, and by the refinement of his taste. With the synthetic power of Dante, and with the analytical faculties of Thomas Aquinas, his mind embraced all human knowledge in its unity and universality, with the view of erecting a philosophical encyclopædia which was to be derived from one principle and divided into different branches, according to their logical order. Of this encyclopædia he published some twenty volumes, in which science is founded on a new and immovable basis, and developed with such a deep, broad, and original survey, that few philosophers, either in ancient or modern times, can be compared to him in this respect. In his religious feelings, though a sincere believer and enlightened apostle of the Catholic church, in which he was born and educated, yet he did not approve, nay openly condemned the excesses of the clergy, and whatever abuses he might have found in the church. Hence the severe trials to which he was submitted under the influence of extreme parties of both sides. But the strictness of Rosmini's life, and the holy charity with which he was endowed, secured him the blessedness which arises from the contemplation of truth and the practice of benevolence. Tolerant of all opinions, and respectful to all men, though dissenting from him, despising all honors which the world could bestow upon him, giving up to charitable objects the large fortune which he had inherited from his family, Rosmini showed himself a true follower of him, in the faith of whom he lived and died. He ended his life in 1855, at Stresa, on the Lago Maggiore, at the age of fifty-eight years." See "*An account of the system of education and of the institutions of science and art in the kingdom of Sardinia.* By VINCENZO BOTTA, Hartford, 1858.

NOTE E.

The following extract from Macaulay, whose independent character and liberal views give great weight to his authority on this subject, illustrates the bearing of the principle of the Reformation, although but imperfectly developed, on the progress of nations:

"The Protestant boasts, and most justly, that wealth, civilization, and intelligence have increased far more on the northern than on the southern side of the geographical boundary which runs between the two religions; that countries so little favored by nature as Scotland and Prussia are now among the most flourishing and best governed portions of the world, while banditti infest the beautiful shores of Campagna, and the fertile sea-coast of the pontifical states is abandoned to buffaloes and wild boars. It cannot be doubted that since the 16th century the Protestant nations, fair allowance being made for physical disadvantages, have made decidedly greater progress than their neighbors. The progress made by those nations in which Protestantism, though not finally successful, yet maintained a long struggle and left permanent traces, has generally been considerable. When we come to the Catholic land, to the part of Europe in which the first spark of Reformation was trodden out as soon as it appeared, and from which proceeded the impulse which drove Protestantism back, we find, at best, a very slow progress, and on the whole a retrogression. Compare Denmark and Portugal. When Luther began to preach, the superiority of the Portuguese was unquestionable; at present, the superiority of the Danes is no less so. Compare Edinburgh and Florence. Edinburgh has owed less to climate, to soil, and to the fostering care of rulers, than any capital, Protestant or Catholic. In all these respects, Florence has been singularly happy. Yet whoever knows what Florence and Edinburgh were in the generation preceding the Reformation, and what they are now, will acknowledge that some great cause has, during the last three centuries, operated to raise one part of the European family, or to depress the other. Compare the history of England and that of Spain during the last century. In arms, arts, sciences, letters, commerce, agriculture, the contrast is most striking. The distinction is not confined to this side of the Atlantic. The colonies planted by England in America have immeasurably outgrown in power those planted by Spain. Yet we have no reason to believe that at the beginning of the 16th century the Castilian was in any respect inferior to the Englishman. Our firm belief is, that the north owes its great civilization and prosperity chiefly to the moral effect of the Protestant Reformation; and that the decay of the southern countries of Europe is to be mainly ascribed to the great Catholic revival." See *Macaulay* "*On Ranke's History of the Popes.*"

NOTE F.

The following passage from the Divine Comedy, Purgatorio, Canto XXXIII., where Beatrice foretells to Dante the advent of a military leader, *the one sent from God*, who shall redeem the country, and *slay both the foul one* (the papacy), *and the giant, the accomplice of her guilt* (the foreign power which conspired with the popes against national unity), refers with greater propriety to Victor Emmanuel, the representative of the Italian people, than to Can della Scala or any of those ancient chiefs to whom the interpreters of the poem apply it. It is probable that Dante, in this and other similar passages, did not intend to designate any particular leader, but that he only gave expression to that patriotic faith which caused him to believe that some Italian prince would in future arise and become the deliverer of the nation. However this may be, the application of the following prophecy of Beatrice to the first king of Italy seems fully justified:

"Ch' io veggio certamente, e però 'l narro,
A darne tempo già stelle propinque,
Sicuro d' ogni intoppo e d' ogni sbarro;
Nel quale un cinquecento dieci e cinque,
Messo di Dio, anciderà la fuja,
E quel gigante che con lei delinque.

. . . .

Tu nota; e sì come da me son porte
Queste parole, sì le 'nsegna a' vivi
Del viver ch' è un correre alla morte."

CONCLUDING NOTE.

The January number of the "Rivista Contemporanea," of Turin, 1862, received since this discourse has been in press, contains a series of Cavour's letters now for the first time published. These letters were mostly addressed to his friend Rattazzi, and are particularly interesting, as illustrating the personal and political character of the writer. Among them, those written during the Congress of Paris, 1856, relate to his private discussions of the Italian question with the Emperor Napoleon, Lord Clarendon, and the leading statesmen of the day, and prove that it was chiefly due to the firm and bold position taken by Cavour that those diplomats admitted at last, the necessity of a war against Austria; that England gave to Italy her moral support, and the Emperor decided to take an active part in the struggle. Of Napoleon, Cavour speaks as follows:—"He fully sympathizes with Italy; and whenever he sees a necessity for decisive measures, he will act with that energy which so distinguishes his character. He is not opposed to the war; on the contrary, he longs for it with all his heart." From these letters it appears also that Cavour identified the cause of the pope with that of Austria, and that in his mind the fate of the one was entirely connected with that of the other. "If we put ourselves in direct relation with Rome," says he, "we shall completely ruin the whole edifice which we have so ardently striven to rear. We cannot preserve our influence in Italy, if we reconcile ourselves with the pontiff. We must fight Austria in Bologna and Rome, as well as in Venice and Milan."

For the institutions of the United States, Cavour had the highest admiration; and while the statesmen of England have so signally failed to appreciate the true issue of the contest which has menaced the national existence of a great people allied to the English nation by race and language, he from the beginning expressed an intelligent sympathy for the free States, in their present contest for constitutional liberty and nationality. This brief tribute to his memory could not be more properly concluded than by quoting the following extract from his last despatch addressed to Chevalier Bertinatti, the minister of Italy at Washington, on the 22d of May, 1861, only a few days before his death:—

"You will continue to hold with the legal government of the federal union, those friendly relations to which they have acquired a new title by their prompt and generous recognition of the kingdom of Italy. At the same time you will maintain a strict reserve toward the parties which divide the confederation. But this reserve, Monsieur le Chevalier, will not prevent us from manifesting our sympathies for the triumph of the Northern States; for their cause is the cause not only of constitutional liberty, but of all humanity. Christian Europe cannot wish success to a party which bears on its standard the preservation and extension of slavery, and which, re-establishing letters of marque and privateering, calls into its service a principle condemned alike by human conscience and modern civilization. Our most sincere and ardent wish would be for an honorable agreement, which, reuniting the States momentarily separated, should extinguish the torch of civil war in a country, whose liberty and prosperity formed but now the admiration of the whole world."

CAVOUR.

To complete the present publication the following correspondence in reference to it is subjoined:

New York, *February* 10th, 1862.

Professor Botta :—*Dear Sir :* Understanding that you have prepared a discourse on the life and policy of the late Count Cavour, it would gratify the undersigned, as well as many others among your fellow-citizens, if you would give them an opportunity of hearing it, and testifying their respect for the memory of the great statesman of Italy, whose name has become identified with the cause of civil and religious liberty. We are very respectfully yours,

George Opdyke (*Mayor of the city of New York*).
Luther Bradish (*President of the Historical Society*).
F. De Peyster (*Vice-President of the Historical Society*).
G. H. Moore (*Librarian of the Historical Society*).
Ch. King (*President of the Columbia College*).
Isaac Ferris (*Chancellor of the University of New York*).
Horace Webster (*Principal of the Free Academy*).
Francis Lieber (*Professor in the Columbia College, and corresponding Member of the Institute of France*).
George Bancroft. W. C. Bryant.
George Folsom. Ch. Butler.
Samuel F. B. Morse. Henry T. Tuckerman.
James W. Beekman.

PROFESSOR BOTTA'S REPLY.

New York, *February* 17th, 1862.

Gentlemen :—I am honored and gratified in receiving your invitation to deliver a discourse commemorative of the great statesman to whom my country is chiefly indebted for its national existence, and whose achievements form so brilliant an episode in contemporary history. I shall be most happy to comply with your request.

I am, with great respect,
Your obedient servant, V. Botta.

To the Hon. George Opdyke, Mayor of the city of New York, and others.

At the close of the discourse, the following resolutions offered by Rev. J. P. Thompson, D. D. were unanimously adopted:

Resolved, That the thanks of this meeting be tendered to Professor Vincenzo Botta, for his instructive and discriminating discourse upon the character and services of Count Cavour, and that, in view of its permanent historical interest and value, he be requested to prepare the same for the press in the English, French, and Italian tongues.

Resolved, That the disinterested patriotism, the enlightened statesmanship, the earnest and consistent devotion to civil and religious liberty, that marked the career of Count Cavour, place him among the noblest champions of political freedom, and of social progress, order, and virtue, through constitutional law; and that his rare administrative capacity exercised for these ends, entitles him to the praise of the regenerator of Italy.

Resolved, That, as the name of this moral leader in the development of the free and enlightened nationality of Italy belongs not to his country only, but to mankind, we claim a fraternal inheritance with the Italian nation in the memory of Cavour, and will gladly unite with them in an appropriate monument to his fame.

Resolved, That while our own experience is teaching us anew, that the stability of free institutions demands the political and moral *unity* of a nation geographically and historically one, we desire the more earnestly the perfecting of that Italian unity which the genius and sagacity of Cavour so happily inaugurated.

Resolved, That since the preservation of national unity under free institutions demands the removal of whatever system or policy is antagonistic to the rights of person or of conscience, the Italian government and nation will have our earnest moral support in their endeavors to terminate all foreign dominion and all politico-ecclesiastical government upon their soil, and to bring the entire population of Italy under a constitution of perfect civil and religious freedom.

This discourse was by request repeated before the New York Athenæum Association, March 12, and before the Boston Young Men's Association on the 19th of the same month, 1862.

www.ingramcontent.com/pod-product-compliance
Lightning Source LLC
LaVergne TN
LVHW021428110826
845150LV00007B/2134

* 9 7 8 1 4 2 5 5 0 7 4 0 4 *